CAMOUFLAGE & MARKINGS
JAROSŁAW WRÓBEL

Luftwaffe
1935·45

part 2

AJ·PRESS

CAMOUFLAGE AND MARKINGS 2

AVAILABLE

AIRCRAFT MONOGRAPH 1
Su-15 FLAGON

AIRCRAFT MONOGRAPH 2
HEINKEL He 111

AIRCRAFT MONOGRAPH 3
MESSERSCHMITT Bf 110

FORTHCOMING TITLES

AIRCRAFT MONOGRAPH 4
Fw 190 A/F/G, PART 1
AIRCRAFT MONOGRAPH 5
Fw 190 A/F/G, PART 2
AIRCRAFT MONOGRAPH 6
Ju 87 STUKA

CAMOUFLAGE AND MARKINGS
LUFTWAFFE 1935-45, PT.1

FORTHCOMING TITLES

LUFTWAFFE 1935-45, PT.2
LUFTWAFFE 1935-45, PT.3

IF YOU WISH TO RECEIVE OUR FREE CATALOGUE LISTING 1000s OF TITLES ON AVIATION, MARITIME AND MILITARY SUBJECTS PLEASE SEND YOUR REQUEST TO:
BOOKS INTERNATIONAL
69B LYNCHFORD RD, FARNBOROUGH, HAMPSHIRE GU14 6EJ, ENGLAND

COPYRIGHT © – A.J.–PRESS – 1995
P. O. Box 28
81–209 GDYNIA 9
POLAND
Tel. & Fax. (+48 58) 20-18-77

English Edition:

BOOKS INTERNATIONAL
69B Lynchford Road
Farnborough, Hampshire GU14 6EJ, England
Telephone: 01252-376564, Fax: 01252-370181

Redaktor naczelny: **Adam Jarski**
Editor in Chief: **Jarosław Wróbel**
Cover painting: **Jarosław Wróbel**
Colour Plates: **Arkadiusz Wróbel, Sławomir Zajączkowski**
Book Design: **Jarosław Wróbel, A.J.–PRESS**
Translations: **Wojtek Matusiak**
Assistant Editor: **Barry Ketley**
Drawings: **Arkadiusz Wróbel, Witold Hazuka, Jarosław Wróbel**
English Edition edited by: **Barry Ketley**
Printed in Poland by: **Drukarnia Oruńska,**
  Gdańsk, ul. Małomiejska 41, tel. (+48 58) 394122

ISBN–83–86208–14–7

BOOKS INTERNATIONAL SALES TEAM AND TERRITORIES
POLAND

BOOKS INTERNATIONAL
ul. LUBELSKA 30-32
03-308 WARSZAWA
POLAND
Tel. & Fax +48 2 619 60 57

FRANCE, SWITZERLAND, HUNGARY, CZECH & SLOVAK REPUBLICS

Mr. Juliusz Komarnicki
CP 196
CH–6900 MASSAGNO
SWITZERLAND
Tel.: +41 - 91 - 57 15 39, Fax: +41 - 91 - 56 78 65

GREECE, ITALY, PORTUGAL, SPAIN (INC. GIB.), SLOVENIA & CROATIA

Mr. Patrick Bygate
CP 196
CH–6900 MASSAGNO
SWITZERLAND
Tel.: +41 - 91 - 57 15 39, Fax: +41 - 91 - 56 78 65

NORDIC GROUP OF COUNTRIES

Mr. Ove B. Poulsen
OPB MARKETING
Hegnet 13
DK-2600 GLOSTRUP
DENMARK
Tel. & Fax: +45 - 43 - 96 50 60

GERMANY, AUSTRIA

Mr. Robert Pleysier
Walkottelanden 72
NL-7542 ENSCHEDE
THE NETHERLANDS
Tel.: +31 - 53 - 77 53 77, Fax: +31 - 53 - 77 82 98

NATHERLANDS, BELGIUM & LUXEMBOURG

Mr. Reinier Pleysier
Kerkdijk 21
PO Box 166
NL-8180 AD HERRE
THE NETHERLANDS
Tel.: +31 - 5782 - 5203, Fax: +31 - 5782 - 5243

OFFENSIVE "GREY" CAMOUFLAGE

The air fighting of 1940 brought many changes in the camouflage patterns of military aircraft on both sides. Both the Germans and the British started introducing camouflage with prevailing grey tones. This reflected the need to hide the aircraft in the air (the so—called "offensive" camouflage). In 1941 the British replaced Dark Earth with Ocean Grey which showed a bluish hue, while retaining Dark Green as the basic camouflage colour. Similarly, the Luftwaffe replaced the Schwarzgrün RLM 70 black—green on fighter Bf 109s and destroyer

Fw 190 A W.Nr. 5735 "red 12" of 8./JG 2 "Richthofen" (1942). The "grey" type camouflage is covered with RLM 74/75 areas, sides and undersurfaces are painted RLM 76. Rudder and lower engine cowling in red.

(P. Jarrett via B. Ketley)

Middle: A damaged Fw 190 A–2 without tail wheel presents Luftwaffe new standard "grey" camouflage. On the fuselage sides is radio—call signs which were painted in factory and used unil the aircraft was transferred to operational unit.

(MVT via M. Krzyżan)

Particulary clear splinter camouflage pattern on the destroyer (Zerstorer) Me 210 A-1. According to the factory scheme this should be comprise two shades of grey - RLM 74 and 75, but in the photo the contrast between the colours is such that the lighter shade could be RLM 76 or RLM 77 rather than RLM 75.

(MVT via M. Krzyżan)

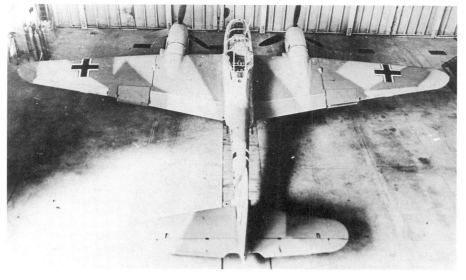

(Zerstörer) Bf 110s with the Grau RLM 02 grey. In the early months of war the basic camouflage was made up of areas in Dunkelgrün RLM 71 (dark green) and Schwarzgrün RLM 70 (black- green) on top surfaces with Hellblau RLM 65 (light blue) undersurfaces. So painted an aircraft was too visible in the air — its dark silhouette was contrasted against the sky — yet it remained well hidden on the ground. That is why this camouflage continued to be used on bomber, transport and reconnaissance aircraft until the end of the war.

Luftwaffe bombers in the "green" camouflage patterns, dispersed on airfields (most often near woods which offered excellent hides for the aircraft from the British

From 1941 on the Luftwaffe introduced "grey" camouflage schemes on fighter aircraft — the photographs show an Fw 190A in a factory camouflage: upper surfaces painted shades of grey ; the darker was RLM 74, and the brighter — RLM 75. Under surfaces and sides of the fuselage were painted RLM 76, with spots of RLM 02 and RLM 74 on the sides only. Propeller spinners was painted blackgreen (RLM 70) with white (RLM 21) quarter. On the fuselage s factory callsigns.

(MVT via M. Krzyżan)

A perfect flying shot of a Messerschmitt Bf 110 C–1, VC+DP, giving a good view of the "grey" camouflage - upper wing and tail surfaces in RLM 74/75 fuselage sides covered in irregular areas of RLM 70/74/02. The photo was taken at the turn of 1940.

(P. Jarrett via B. Ketley)

PR aircraft), merged well against the background without the need for any additional masking such as tree branches.

In the case of fighter and destroyer aircraft the matter was more complicated — the attacking fighter should be least visible both against the sky and the ground. "Grey" paint shades combining the green RLM 71 with the grey RLM 02 seemed a good solu-

An example of simultaneous use of two typical camouflage patterns in the same unit — I./ZG 2, during fighting in 1940. The nearest aeroplane is in the pre-war scheme of RLM 70/71/65, albeit with the new Balkenkreuz type featuring wide white elements. The Messerschmitt Bf 110C in the background is in the new type of painting, with light-coloured fuselage sides (RLM 65) covered with darker areas (RLM 02), fuselage top and upper surfaces are in RLM 02/72. Individual code letters "G" and "H" were red with white outline.

(P. Jarrett via B. Ketley)

Above: A Bf 110 E–1 of 6./ZG 1, 2J+AP, with a crew of three. The aircraft is painted with standard "grey" camouflage RLM 74/75/76.

(P. Jarrett via B. Ketley)

Bf 110 C–5 of 4.(F)/14 "Münchhausen — Staffel" in the RLM 74/75/76 camouflage. On the fuselage is the unit emblem — Baron Münchhausen.

(MVT via M. Krzyżan)

Fw 190 A-4 "white 7" flown by Obfhr. Helmut Wenk of Ergangzungsstaffel SKG 10, Northern France, May 1943. Camouflage of RLM 74/75/76. Note the "white 7" and circle to the right of the cross.

(MVT via M. Krzyżan)

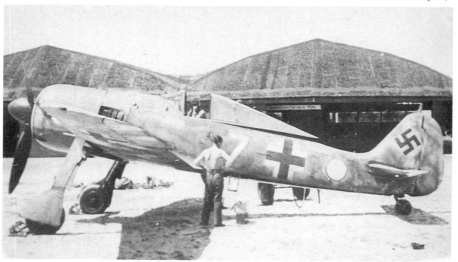

tion here. Additionally fuselage sides were painted RLM 65 — a brighter shade of blue, which was sometimes covered with an irregular mottle of grey RLM 02 and black — green RLM 70 (ranging from a fine stipple applied with a brush, as was the case in JG 2, to large fields, as in JG 53). Such a scheme made the aircraft at an airfield much more conspicuous from the air. This was cured by additional masking of aircraft on the ground with camouflage nets attached to poles around the aeroplane, tree branches or even entire trees. The branches were supported against wing leading edges to dissipate or deform the shadow of the wing — thus completely changing the geometry of the object. Once the problem of camouflaging the aircraft on the ground was solved, the offensive camouflage patterns could be introduced widely. Numerous combinations of the top surface colours were tested. In late summer and early autumn 1940 many German fighters were forced to land on British soil. Each such landing was documented in detail by the RAF. Reports gave precise data of the aircraft type, its markings and camouflage, which was important for the identification of fighter units used against Britain. The German aircraft carried full Geschwader, Gruppe and Staffel markings — colour, characters and graphic symbols enabled identification of the unit. Reports gave detailed descriptions of the markings and camouflage colours — the range of the latter was very wide: "green", "green—grey", "grey", "blue—grey" — all described upper surface colours.

A He 111 H on factory airfield sporting a fresh RLM 70/71/65 camouflage with well visible pattern while factory callsign NO+GP and number 3107 on the fuselage. The wing light grey walkway marking and stencilling near engines is visible.

(MVT via M. Krzyżan)

It is known that as early as May 1940 most Messerschmitt Bf 109s and some Bf 110s wore a two—tone pattern of dark green RLM 71 and grey RLM 02, with blue—grey RLM 65 on lower and side surfaces. The remaining aircraft (for example, Ju 87, Do 17, Ju 52, Hs 126 etc.) retained the camouflage of green shades on their upper surfaces (RLM 70/RLM 71) and blue on lower (RLM 65).

Following earlier experiments, the scheme of RLM 71/02/65, then in use on Luftwaffe fighters was gradually replaced from the turn of 1940 by a combination of Dunkelgrau RLM 74 (dark grey—green) and Grauviolett RLM 75 (grey—mauve), on upper surfaces of wings, tailplanes and fuselage spine, and Hellgrau RLM 76 (blue—grey), on wing and tailplane under-surfaces as well as fuselage lower and undersides. Fuselage sides also received an irregular pattern of grey—green RLM 02 and black—green RLM 70 mottling. This practice was formalised in the orders contained within the L.Dv. 521 (LuftDruckvorschrift — Air Regulation) of November 1941, a detailed account of which follows later.

In the summer of 1942 Messerschmitt Bf 109 Gs left the assembly lines in a "grey" camouflage of RLM 74/75/76, their sides mottled with RLM 02/70/74, the propeller spinners were painted with three colours: RLM 21/70/76. The aircraft on the factory airfield have their radio — call signs painted in black, these would be overpainted upon arrival in the unit. Note the interesting variations to the wing Balkenkreuz — the aircraft in the foreground have their crosses according to the new standard, while the third in line has the old type cross (with the black "core").

(P. Jarrett via B. Ketley)

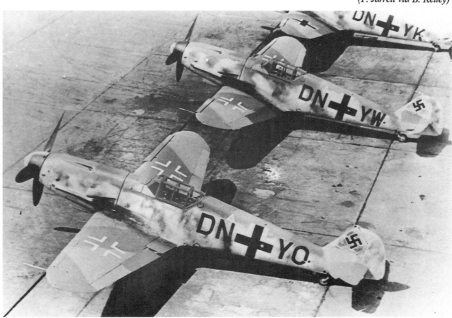

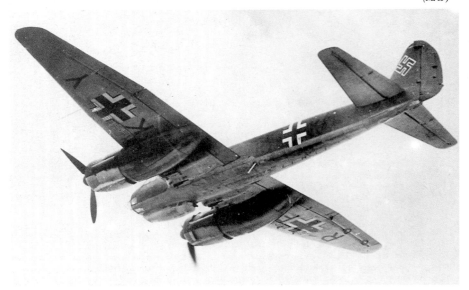

Above: Reconnaissance Junkers 88D–2 — with camera ports visible under the fuselage. Fuselage and wings display the callsign. Near the fuselage Balkenkreuz sharp splinter division lines between the RLM 70/71/65 colours.

(MAP)

Above: Ju 88A–4 bomber during a test flight on one engine with clearly visible positioning of national markings and code letters.

(MAP)

Below: Do 215B–1 bomber, ND+TB,1940. National markings are clearly visible, as are the letters of the radio callsign on wings and fuselage. Aircraft in the RLM 70/71/65 camouflage.

(A. Jarski coll.)

CODES AND QUICK RECOGNITION MARKINGS

On leaving the factory every aircraft received — apart from the camouflage — a radio call sign code for communications during ferry flights. The code consisted of four letters (for example, KB+PV) painted in black or white on each fuselage side so that the Balkenkreuz was positioned between the second and third character. The code was repeated on wing undersurfaces in black. Upon arrival in the unit the code was overpainted with camouflage colours and was replaced with standard combat markings — in the case of single–engined fighters this was a number within the range 1 to 15, in the Staffel colour (to one side of the fuselage cross) and the Gruppe symbol in the same colour (on the other side of the cross). An aircraft could also receive a function marking such as chevrons or bars, depending upon the function of the pilot within the unit. On multi–engined fighters, bombers, reconnaissance, training and transport aircraft appropriate codes were applied. For example; M8+FH on a Bf 110 of 1./ZG 26, where "M8" meant ZG 26; the next character — "F" in this case, which was painted or outlined in the Staffel colour, here white, — was an individual letter for each aircraft, and the character "H" identified the Staffel within the Geschwader — in this case the 1.Staffel.

The radio call sign on wing undersurfaces was usually overpainted. It happened, however, that sometimes it was left unchanged or only partly overpainted by applying combat codes over the radio call sign. An example is a Messerschmitt Bf 109G that belonged to the ace Lt. Erich Hartmann of 7./JG 52, that carried both the black radio call sign KJ+GJ (K+J on the starboard wing undersurface, G+J on the port wing) and the combat number "2" +"wave" applied on the fuselage.

The combat codes were painted with standard RLM paints (as described in Table No. 1). There were rare exceptions to this standard, for instance 6 Staffel of JG 26 used brown numbers in September 1940, reason for this was probably better concealment.

The same colours were used to paint other types of markings, for example: to paint propeller spinners in Staffel colours, as well as to paint other elements, like engine cowlings, rudders, fuselage bands etc. The colour of identification markings varied

He 111 bombers of 6./KG 1 "Hindenburg", 1940. The black cross on the fuselage of V4+IP is very visible. The individual letter was yellow. The wing undersides show traces of overpainted factory radio call signs (lighter areas) while on the starboard portion the "I", individual letter, was applied next to the Balkenkreuz.

(R. Michulec coll.)

Table No. 1

COLOURS OF COMBAT AND IDENTYFICATION CODES PAINTED ON LUFTWAFFE AIRCRAFT	
RKM COLOUR	CODE
RLM 24 (blue)	individual letters of Geschwader Staff aircraft with four – character codes.
RLM 25 (green)	individual letters of Gruppe Staff aircraft with four – character codes.
RLM 21 (white)	individual letters or numbers in 1., 4., 7., 10. and 13. Staffel.
RLM 23 (red)	individual letters or numbers in 2., 5., 8., 11. and 14. Staffel
RLM 27 RLM 04 (yellow)	individual letters or numbers in 3., 6., 9., 12., 15. Staffel.
RLM 22 (black)	the remaining characters in four–character codes on all aircraft except the single–engined fighters (occasionally black was used instead of the red RLM 23).

Above: Prototype Ju 88 V44 (NF+KQ) converted to the Ju 188 V1. The picture shows well the positions of Balkenkreuzes (without the thin outline) and code letters — N+F under the starboard wing and K+Q under the port one.

(MVT via M. Krzyżan)

Below: A group of transport Junkers Ju 52/3m 4mge aircraft of KG zbV 172 on a Greek airfield, spring 1941, during the battle of Crete. The aircraft nose in the foreground features the unit emblem (white deer) and yellow engine cowling. Camouflage of RLM 70/71/65. In the background two more Ju 52s, also with yellow cowlings and rudders, typical markings during the Balkan campaign in 1941.

(R. Michulec coll)

among units and theatres. During the Battle of Britain the most common quick recognition markings were yellow or white noses, rudders and wing tips. These enabled rapid identification in a dogfight. It was all too easy to shoot down a friendly aircraft (which, albeit rarely, happened on both sides). The I. Gruppe C.O. in Jagdgeschwader 3 (JG 3), Hptm. Hans von Hahn, flew a Messerschmitt Bf 109 E–4 in the autumn of 1940, which while retaining the then standard camouflage of RLM 71/02/65 also featured a yellow nose as far back as the windscreen and a yellow rudder. The spinner of the fighter was painted in the typical style for 1940 — half in the factory colour of black–green RLM 70, the other half in white RLM 21, which was a Gruppe marking. Additionally the very tip of the spinner was green RLM 25, which identified the aircraft as belonging to the C.O. To further reinforce the point the Geschwader "Tatzelwurm" badge was applied in green. Other aircraft sported the badge in Gruppe colours (white in I. Gruppe, red in II. and yellow in III.).

PATTERNS OF PROPELLER SPINNERS ON GERMAN FIGHTERS IN 1940–43.

THE BASIC RULE WAS TO PAINT A PORTION OF THE SPINNER IN THE STAFFEL COLOUR YELLOW (RLM 04), WHITE (RLM 21), RED (RLM 23) OR GREEN (RLM 25)

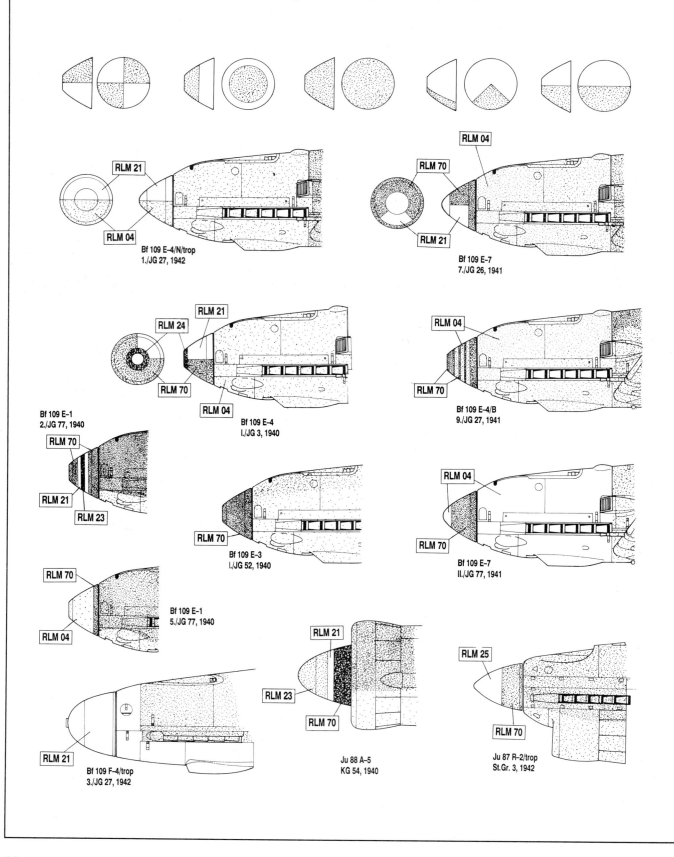

RLM 21 / RLM 04
Bf 109 E-4/N/trop
1./JG 27, 1942

RLM 04 / RLM 70 / RLM 21
Bf 109 E-7
7./JG 26, 1941

RLM 21 / RLM 24 / RLM 70 / RLM 04
Bf 109 E-1
2./JG 77, 1940

Bf 109 E-4
I./JG 3, 1940

RLM 04 / RLM 70
Bf 109 E-4/B
9./JG 27, 1941

RLM 70 / RLM 21 / RLM 23

RLM 70
Bf 109 E-3
I./JG 52, 1940

RLM 04 / RLM 70
Bf 109 E-7
II./JG 77, 1941

RLM 70 / RLM 04
Bf 109 E-1
5./JG 77, 1940

RLM 21
Bf 109 F-4/trop
3./JG 27, 1942

RLM 21 / RLM 23 / RLM 70
Ju 88 A-5
KG 54, 1940

RLM 25 / RLM 70
Ju 87 R-2/trop
St.Gr. 3, 1942

EXAMPLES OF SPIRALS ON SPINNERS OF LUFTWAFFE FIGHTER AIRCRAFT FROM 1943.

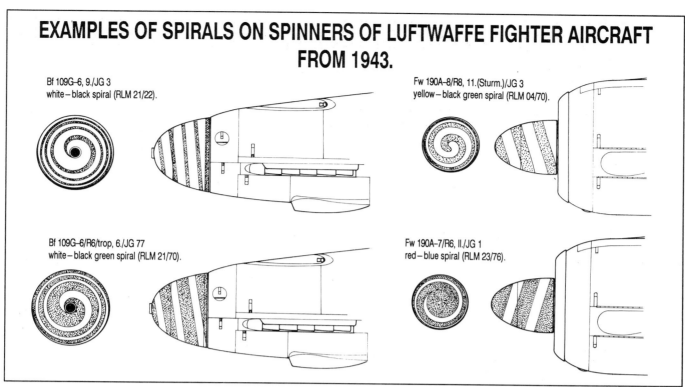

Bf 109G–6, 9./JG 3
white – black spiral (RLM 21/22).

Fw 190A–8/R8, 11.(Sturm.)/JG 3
yellow – black green spiral (RLM 04/70).

Bf 109G–6/R6/trop, 6./JG 77
white – black green spiral (RLM 21/70).

Fw 190A–7/R6, II./JG 1
red – blue spiral (RLM 23/76).

QUICK IDENTIFICATION ELEMENTS ON LUFTWAFFE FIGHTER AIRCRAFT 1940 – 43.

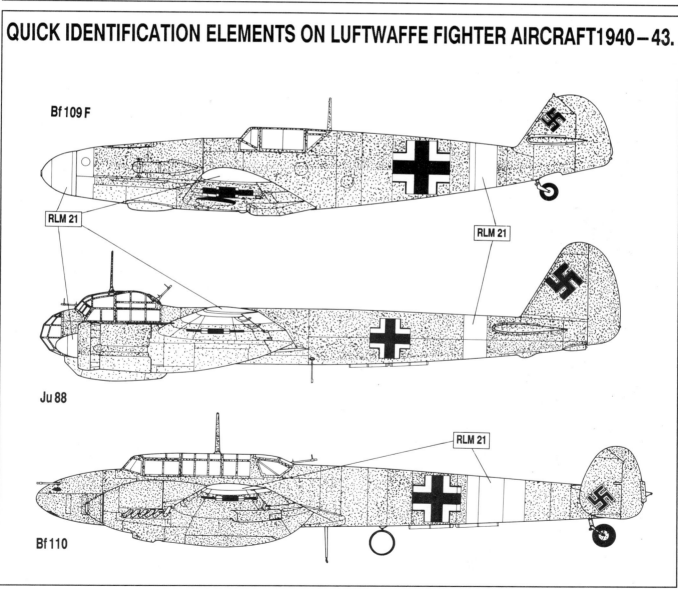

Bf 109 F

RLM 21

RLM 21

Ju 88

RLM 21

Bf 110

TYPICAL POSITIONING OF YELLOW (RLM 04) RAPID IDENTIFICATION ELEMENTS OF LUFTWAFFE AIRCRAFT DURING THE BALKAN CAMPAIGN, SPRING 1941.

Ju 88 A

Ju 52 3m

Bf 109 E

Ju 87 B

TYPICAL LUFTWAFFE AIRCRAFT MARKINGS IN THE MEDITERRANEAN THEATRE IN 1941–43.

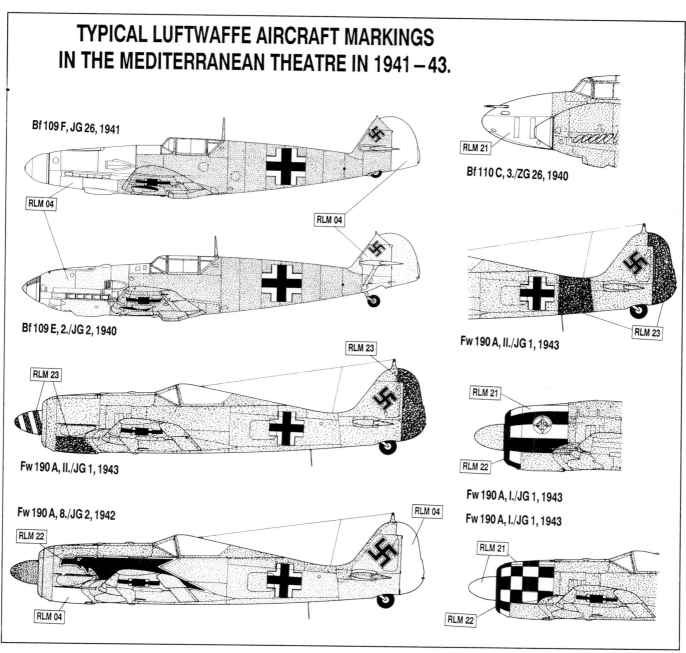

Bf 109 F, JG 26, 1941

RLM 04

RLM 04

Bf 109 E, 2./JG 2, 1940

RLM 23

RLM 23

Fw 190 A, II./JG 1, 1943

Fw 190 A, 8./JG 2, 1942

RLM 22

RLM 04

RLM 04

Bf 110 C, 3./ZG 26, 1940

RLM 21

Fw 190 A, II./JG 1, 1943

RLM 23

RLM 21

RLM 22

Fw 190 A, I./JG 1, 1943
Fw 190 A, I./JG 1, 1943

RLM 21

RLM 22

VARIOUS FORMS OF NON–STANDARD JG 2 EMBLEM APPLIED TO FW 190As IN 1942–43.

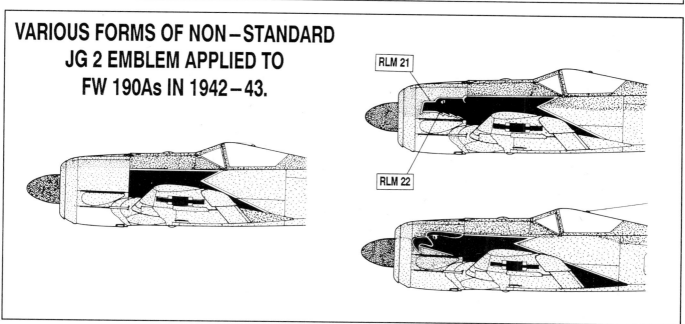

RLM 21

RLM 22

A pilot leaves his Messerschmitt Bf 110 after a sortie. On the fuselage is visible the emblem of 7. Staffel ZG 26, North Africa, 1941-1942.
(MVT via M. Krzyżan)

The Bf 109E–4 of Staffelkapitän Oblt. Gerhardt Schopfel of 9./JG 26 "Schlageter" was a good example of 1940 wingtip and tail recognition markings. 44 cm of the wingtips were painted yellow, as were 53 cm of the tailplane tips. Additionally, the top of the rudder, number "1" and vertical bar codes on the fuselage, were all yellow. Another element in the colour of III. Gruppe was the small metal pennant attached to the aerial mast on top of the fuselage. The propeller spinner in Schopfel's mount was in factory—finished black—green RLM 70, without an additional Staffel or Gruppe colour. On the spinners of other aircraft, both in JG 26 and other units, halves, quarters or bands were often painted in Staffel or Gruppe colours.

In 1943 spinners of Bf 109s, Fw 190s and Ju 87s started to be painted with a spiral, most often black or black—green (RLM 70) on the white spinner, less often red (RLM 23), with varying stroke and pitch, i. e. the number of curves. The exact reasons for this treatment are difficult to establish, but it is generally assumed that this was to prevent accurate aiming by Allied gunners during a head—on attack by the Luftwaffe fighters. The rotating spiral was supposed to produce an optical illusion which confused the gunners.

Following their appearance in mid—1940, the use of quick recognition markings soon started an expansion of such elements in other theatres. Yellow—nosed and —tailed fighters took part in the fighting over the English Channel (for example, those of JG 26). During the Balkan campaign in the spring of 1941 they still had their noses and tails in yellow. Almost immediately all the aircraft in that theatre, even bombers and reconnaissance aircraft, received yellow quick identification markings. i.e. RLM 04 was applied to the fuselage nose in the case of single engined aircraft or engine cowlings on multi—engined types. The yellow paint was also applied to rudders. Such was the scheme of Messerschmitt Bf 109Es of JG 77 in April 1941. The rapid movement of aircraft between different countries during 1941—42 led to many aircraft carrying

Obstlt Schalk, C.O. of ZG 26 standing on the wing of his Bf 110 - the commanders chevron in red outlined in black is applied under the cockpit on the grey fuselage.
(MVT via M. Krzyżan)

markings of different theatres simultaneously. For example, following their arrival in North Africa in April 1941, aircraft from JG 26 received a white band around the rear fuselage, in line with their Italian allies, as well as retaining the yellow tactical markings used over the Channel. In the spring of 1941 Staffelkapitän Oblt. Joachim Müncheberg flew a Bf 109E–7/N while with the Sicily—based 7./JG 26. His aircraft sported "grey" camouflage, as tested over the Channel — RLM75/74 on top surfaces and RLM 76 on lower ones. Müncheberg's aircraft had a yellow nose and rudder, white fuselage band, white "12" and two badges; that of JG 26, a black gothic "S" on a white shield, placed in the standard position under the cockpit and a "red heart" 7. Staffel emblem applied to the upper engine cowling. Propeller spinner was black—green (RLM 70) with a white quarter and white tip to denote the Staffel. The aerial mast pennant was also in the same colour. Fuselage and underwing crosses featured wide white elements, while the crosses on top of the wing were 'narrow' types of 1936 standard, which remained unchanged until the end of the war on many Luftwaffe aircraft. Swastika was in the standard position, in the middle of the fin. Yellow rudder sported 33 black kill markings.

The Balkans also saw other types of aircraft with markings typical for the theatre. Even though later on the Eastern Front yellow identification elements were also used, the Balkan markings can be easily distinguished from those of the Russian Front. First of all, in the Balkans yellow bands around the rear fuselage were extremely rare, while these were the rule in Russia. On the other hand, rudders were not usually painted yellow on the Eastern Front. Yellow was seldom applied to engine cowlings, and even if it was then only in small amounts. This is best testified to by Stuka paint schemes — if a photograph shows a Ju 87 with a yellow (i. e. bright in a black—and—white photo) nose and rudder then it is almost certain that it shows an aircraft during the Balkans campaign. For example, Junkers Ju 87B–2 of 5./StG 77, S2+LN, carried typical theatre markings: yellow engine cowlings (those easily removable, for example for an engine check), yellow rudder and wingtip undersurfaces. The camouflage on upper surfaces was black—green RLM 70 (no RLM 71 areas), and undersurfaces were standard blue RLM 65. The aircraft belonged to 5. Staffel, the colour of which

Above: Messerschmitts of III./JG 52 pictured in 1940. The wavy line between the cross on the fuselage and the fin is the III. Gruppe marking. The "grey" camouflage pattern is well visible as are the darker (RLM 70) areas on fuselage sides. White nose, band around the fuselage, rudder and wingtips - are all quicke identification markings.
(P. Jarrett via B. Ketley)

Below: Ju 87 B of 3./StG 3, Bakans, Spring 1941. the aircraft is in typical camouflage of RLM 70/71/65 with yellow quick identification markings, typical for the Balkan campaign.
(P. Jarrett via B. Ketley)

Below: Loading drop canisters onto Junkers Ju 52 transport aircraft, probably during the battle of Crete, spring 1941. Yellow engine cowlings and rudders, typical for the Balkan campaign.
(R. Michulec coll.)

Above: A pair of Bf 110Ds with increased fuel tanks under wings - the aircraft belonged to the III./ZG 26 and operated in 1942 over North Africa, but still they carried "European" camouflage of RLM 74/75/76.

(MVT via M. Krzyżan)

Above: Taking off from a dusty airfield is a Bf 109F-4 of III./JG 53 "Pik As" in typical Mediterranean markings - white nose, fuselage band and wingtips. The unit emblem on cowling, on the white band a vertical bar - III. Gruppe emblem.

(P. Jarrett via B. Ketley)

Jagdfliegerschulen (flying training units) used, among others, the Arado Ar 68E. The one in the photo bears the 70/71/65 camouflage, and black code RB+B25 on the fuselage. The 1 meter-wide white band around the fuselage and on the upper wing centre section was a tipical marking of the training aircraft.

(MVT via M. Krzyżan)

was red, consequently that was the colour of the fourth code latter ("L") on the fuselage, which also featured a white outline to better stand out against the dark background. Also half of the spinner was painted in the Staffel colour. Like all the bombers of that Geschwader, this aircraft sported the Staffel badge, but no Geschwader emblem. Several weeks later Stukas of this unit were moved to the Russian Front, where the yellow noses and rudders were overpainted, while a yellow fuselage band was applied right behind the cross.

When writing about the aircraft of the Balkan campaign it should be noted that as time went by, the yellow identification elements — applied to most aircraft — were supplemented with white elements, following the markings conventions of Italy's Regia Aeronautica. These comprised white wingtips, fuselage bands and white propeller spinners.

White fuselage bands were applied on some Messerschmitt Bf 109s of JG 26, He 111s of KG 26 and many others. For example, a Junkers 88A–4, 4D+HT, of III./KG 30 "Adlergeschwader", based in Sicily and taking part in fighting over Greece, featured standard bomber camouflage, which was introduced prior to WWII, in 1938, and remained in use almost until its end in 1945. This consisted of two shades of green (RLM 70 and RLM 71) on upper surfaces and blue—grey (RLM 65) on lower. Both engine cowlings were painted yellow, while the wingtip undersurfaces were white, like on Italian aeroplanes; also the fuselage band was white. The third letter of the black fuselage code, 4D+HT, was — in accordance with the regulations — in the colour of 9. Staffel (yellow), propeller spinners were painted similarly.

An example of the transition to entirely white markings (which could be called "Italian"), typical for later stages of the campaign in Africa and the Mediterranean, is provided by the Heinkel He 111H–3, 1H+MM, of II./KG 26 "Löwengeschwader" in the camouflage of RLM 70/71/65 with white spinners, white fuselage band and white rudder.

Above: Landing mishap to a Stuka (Ju 87B–1) with radio code, NH+GR, in black plus a letter "A" in the Staffel colour (green?).

(P. Jarrett via B. Ketley)

Below: Line of Ju 87B–2 dive bombers of I./StG 2, early spring 1941, prior to the Balkan campaign. On the fuselages the I. Gruppe emblem — black Scotch terrier on a disc in Staffel colour: 1. Staffel — white, 2. Staffel — red, 3. Staffel — yellow, Gruppenstab — blue.

(P. Jarrett via B. Ketley)

He 111H, T5+AU of Wekusta ObdL. Traces of over painted factory code and a small pre-war type Balkenkreuz (close to the wingtip) are visible. These were replaced by new A+U codes with a now wider Balkenkreuz.

(MVT via M. Krzyżan)

LDv. 521/2

1941 was the year of the consequences of the lost Battle of Britain; the year of the campaigns in the Balkans and in Africa; the year the war with the USSR started; the year when new fighter types were introduced (Bf 109F and Fw 190) and also the year when new camouflage colours for fighter aircraft were formally introduced into the Luftwaffe. These were three grey tones: Dunkelgrau RLM 74, Grauviolett RLM 75 and Hellblau RLM 76. All were previously used to paint Messerschmitt Bf 109Es. From November 1941 the factory fresh Bf 109Fs were painted according to the official LDv.

A Klemm Kl 35D training two-seater in light grey RLM 63.

(P. Jarrett via B. Ketley)

521/2 Regulations. RLM 74 was a dark grey shade of green, brighter than the previously used RLM 71. RLM 74 was accompanied on upper surfaces by RLM 75 which — much lighter — was a shade somewhere between a grey tone with a slight blue or blue—mauve hue (some British eye—witness reports following forced landings of German fighters describe this as a "dirty blue"). On lower and side surfaces, blue—grey RLM 76 was applied, which did not differ much from the previously used RLM 65. This is why it cannot be ascertained with certainty exactly what colour was used on the lower surfaces of Messerschmitt Bf 109Es painted before August 1941 — were

they RLM 74/75/76, or RLM 74/75/65? The regulations introduced new paint for lower surfaces, but since the two shades were so similar (RLM 76 was slightly more grey), it has to be said that probably these were used in parallel. Since bombers and other military types continued to be painted in the "old" colours of RLM 70/71/65, the RLM 76 — for practical reasons — must have been compatible with RLM 65. The "old" RLM 70 and RLM 02 shades were still used in the new scheme — to apply irregular patterns on fuselage sides.

Regulations for military aircraft painting schemes, as numerous as they were, described in much detail not only paint shades but also the areas of their application, using for that purpose special diagrams — line—grids which provided reference for the paint shops. For example, LDv 553/2 referred to the Dornier Do 17F, LDv 553/3 — Do 17M, LDv 553/4 — Do 17P. These were printed as a manual with several chapters — general description of the painting; detailed painting descriptions for the fuselage; wings; landing gear; a chapter about primers; protective coats; number of layers etc., LDv 521/2 was important in that it withdrew from use the RLM 61,62,63 paints. While prohibiting the use of RLM 01 silver on trainer aircraft (probably because the silver was too visible against the ground), a camouflage pattern was suggested without stating the exact colours. In practice the trainers would be painted light grey—green (RLM 02), or in the schemes RLM 70/71/65 and RLM 74/75/76. Fighters

Typical for 1943—1944 early night fighter camouflage, a Do 217 J–2, GE+EA, painted RLM 22 black overall. Only code letters and propeller spinners are RLM 77 grey, whole the Balkenkreuzes and number 51 are white.

(P. Jarrett via B. Ketley)

and destroyers were to be painted RLM 74/75/76; bomber, transport and reconnaissance aircraft were to retain the previous scheme of RLM 70/71/65 and the maritime aircraft — RLM 72/73/65, where RLM 72 and RLM 73 were replacements for RLM 70 and 71 with a slightly blue—grey hue. A novelty in the new regulations were precise instructions on the tropical camouflage shades, Himmelblau RLM 78 (blue) on lower surfaces, Sandgelb RLM 79 (sand—yellow) and Olivgrün RLM 80 (olive—green) on upper surfaces. RLM 79 and

RLM 80 had their earlier variants or so some sources say. However, when it is remembered that the Luftwaffe was conceived as a European air force, and that Hitler had never intended to become embroiled in the Balkans or Mediterranean theatres until he was dragged into them by his Italian ally, then there is strong circumstancial evidence for the use of Italian paints. As early Luftwaffe aircraft in these theatres were rushed there before properly formulated paints, supplies or even uniforms could be issued, then the incentive

to use what was readily available is easily understood. The most likely colours used would be the Italian Giallo Mimetico 4 (Sand Yellow) and Verde Mimetico 3 (Mottle Green) on the uppersurfaces, while it is quite possible that the undersides retained their original Luftwaffe colours, as the contemporary Italian Grigio Azzurro Chiaro 1 is a definite grey. It may well be significant that one of the most important Italian camouflage paints, Nocciola Chiaro (Light Hazel) is an almost exact match to Luftwaffe Sandgelb 79.

MARKING VARIATIONS

LDv 521/2 also introduced some modification to the Balkenkreuz appearance. Upper wing surface crosses had their "inte-

Do 217 N-2, PE+AW, in a non-standart camouflage - under and sides surfaces in RLM 76 blue grey, upper and partly side surfaces (including inner and outer fin and rudder surfaces) in RLM 75 grey. Note the white Balkenkreuz on the fuselage painted on a grey (75) square.

(P. Jarrett via B. Ketley)

Two Junkers 88C–4s (destroyer version) on a factory airfield. Note the sharp camouflage colour division the line of the RLM 70/71/65 scheme. On the fuselage and wings black radio code letters. Balkenkreuz in the form of just the white elements.

(MAP)

rior" removed, so that only the white outline of the cross was left (in practice the old–style Balkenkreuze continued for some time or the cross "interior" was painted with the RLM 74 darker camouflage shade). The rule was also used for the fuselage cross — the wide white outline was filled with dark grey–green RLM 74. Often the traditional black cross was applied, but lacking the nar-row black border to the white elements of the cross. On lower wing surfaces the Balkenkreuze never lost their black "inte-rior" — only the thin outer black outline was omitted, as it was with the swastika — the internal part was always black with white outline. At the very end of the war further changes to Balkenkreuz and Hakenkreuz occurred and these will be described in detail in future books of the Luftwaffe Camouflage and Markings series.

In spite of the introduction of simplified national markings, Messerschmitt Bf 109Fs seldom presented the "grey crosses", usual-ly "Friedrichs" sported Balkenkreuze of the traditional style — for example, in the sum-mer of 1941 the Bf 109F–4 of F. Schies of JG 53 "Pik–As" wore (as did most aircraft of the unit) black fuselage crosses with wide white and narrow black outlines. Similarly shaped crosses were applied on wing lower surfaces, while the crosses on upper wing surface — while retaining the same colours — featured narrower white elements (Balkenkreuz of 1936). Similarly, the cros-ses on Bf 109Fs of other units, for example, in JG 27 which fought in Africa, and its leading ace, Hans–Joachim Marseille, flew a "Friedrich" with black crosses.

Only as late as 1943, and on a later Mes-serschmitt variant — the Bf 109G, did the lighter fuselage Balkenkreuz of RLM 74/21 appear, as did the upper wing surface cros-ses of just the white outline. Most often only the thin black outline to the cross arms were omitted. More radical changes and simplifi-cations were not introduced before the series of "Gustav" G–6s — with modified camouflage pattern (but an unchanged set

A pair of Messerschmitt Bf 110 Es of 7./NJG 4 night fighter unit over Germany (1942). The aircraft are painted black RLM 22 overall grey (RLM 77) codes. The individual letter "G" in white outline (Satffel colour). Under the cockpit, a partly obscured Geschwader emblem - "Englandblitz"

(P. Jarrett via B. Ketley)

A Stuka of Stukageschwader 2 "Immelmann" in flight over the desert in late 1941. The aircraft was in standard "European" camouflage (RLM 70/71/65) with clearly visible lighter elements — rear fuselage, wings, landing gear. Forward fuselage with the cockpit was normally protected on the ground with a sun—proof cover, hence the darker shade of the camouflage. Code T6+EM of 4. Staffel StG 2 is visible on the faded and dusty part of the fuselage. White was the colour of the Staffel; this colour was used on the individual letter "E" on the fuselage and on both landing gear spats.

(P. Jarrett via B. Ketley)

of colours — still RLM 74/75) were produced in 1943. Fuselage crosses on most of these aircraft were dark grey—green (RLM 74) and white (RLM 21), the wing Balkenkreuze plain white, and the underwing ones black with wide white elements and no thin black outline. Such markings were applied, for example, to the mount of Hptm. Jurgen Harder, the Gruppenkommandeur of I./JG 53 fighting in the autumn of 1943 over Sicily and Italy. He flew a G–6/R6 in the RLM 74/75/76 camouflage.

Faster changes to national markings were characteristic for the Focke Wulf Fw 190As. Already in early 1942, aircraft wearing the RLM 74/75/76 camouflage had had the wing crosses reduced to a white outline, and the fuselage crosses with the dark grey—green "interior" of RLM 74. For example, the Fw 190A—3, "black 11", W.Nr. 2387 of 8./JG 2 "Richthofen" based in Southern France in mid—1942 carried such Balkenkreuze on the "grey" camouflage of RLM 74/75/76. It should be stressed here, however, that not all of the Fw 190s in 1942 — 43 featured the simplified Balkenkreuze and Hakenkreuze — there are many instances of earlier type crosses being used. In the

case of bomber and transport aircraft the changes of national markings appearance were even slower — as late as the turn of 1943 simplified crosses were rarely used. They became widespread in 1944. Obviously some photographs show earlier examples of white outline crosses application, for example, on the attack Hs 129s of SchG 1,

where the cross interior was made of the background RLM 70/71 camouflage, or on transport Junkers Ju 52/3s operating over Tunis in late 1942, where just the white elements of the crosses were applied on the fuselage and the top of the wing, the lower surfaces sporting earlier standard markings. Generally, however, bomber, reconnais-

Werner Schroer at the controls of his Bf 109 E-4N/trop, "black 8", of 2./JG 27 in flight over Libyan coast 1941. The aircraft in desert camouflage. Lower and side surfaces RLM 78 blue, upper - RLM 79 sand with irregular RLM 80 olive spots. "Black 8" with red outline, the tail sports four red bars (kill symbols).

(P. Jarrett via B. Ketley)

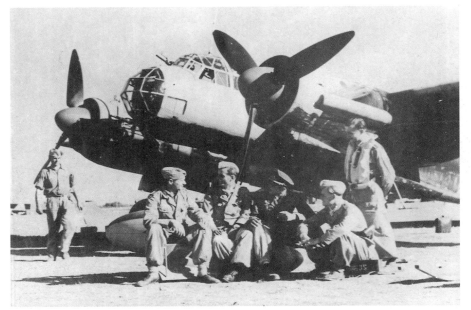

Junkers Ju 88D of 1.(F)/121 with upper surfaces in sand RLM 79 and lower ones in black. The aircraft took part in night missions over North Africa, hence the black camouflage and special flame dampers.

(ADM)

NEW CAMOUFLAGE FOR NIGHT FIGHTING AIRCRAFT

When LDv. 521/2 introduced the new RLM 74/75/76 camouflage schemes for fighters and destroyers, aircraft in night fighter units (Nachtjagdgeschwader — NJG) began to be painted in new grey patterns instead of the previous black camouflage (RLM 22). Some closely resembled the camouflage of day fighting destroyer aircraft, i. e. upper surfaces of wings and tailplanes and fuselage spine were covered with areas of the same colours as for single–engined fighters (RLM 74 and RLM 75). Fuselage sides, fins and rudders, and all lower surfaces were painted RLM 76 with an irregular pattern of RLM 70/02/74/75 blotches on fuselage sides and vertical tails (mottle could be replaced by "scribble" lines, as for example, on a Bf 110G–4 of 7./NJG 3). Messerschmitt Bf 110s camouflaged in this fashion flew both in night fighter and day–time destroyer units. Other schemes could also be encountered, for example when an entire aircraft was painted blue–grey (RLM 76) with only part of the lower surfaces, i.e. starboard wing and sometimes tailplane and starboard half of the fuselage in black (RLM 22). This rare scheme served to identify aircraft of the Beleuchterstaffeln — the so–called illuminator units tasked with dropping parachute flares over the Allied bomber

sance and transport aircraft which continued to use the pre-war camouflage of RLM 70/71/65, also carried the national markings of 1940 standard.

In 1943 Allied raids against target within the Reich intensified. These attacks were countered by Luftwaffe night fighters, the Messerschmitt Bf 110s, Dornier Do 215s, Do 217s and Ju 88s. Since they were in night camouflage of overall black finish, they received the simplified crosses as early as 1941 — the Balkenkreuz colour merged against the black camouflage. Such finishes were applied to NJG 2 aircraft, for example Dornier Do 17Z–6, "Kauz I", R4+HK, — was black overall with only the fuselage code letters in light grey (RLM 77) while the outstanding "H" was in the Staffel colour (red) with a white outline for better visibility against the background.

Ju 87D–1, GP+YA, in a factory applied desert camouflage: top brown–sand RLM 79, bottom is blue RLM 78. White band on the fuselage, black radio code and atypical, sand–coloured propeller spinner and blades (usually painted black green RLM 70).

(P. Jarrett via B. Ketley)

A crew of a Ju 88 A pose to photo in the front of his aircraft, which is painted in "Wellenmuster" schemat. It was used by units operated over the seas.

(M.Griehl coll.)

streams in order to create targets for the single-engined Wilde Sau night fighters. In the summer of 1943 a Bf 110G–2, G9+XR, of 7./NJG 1 wore such a finish with simplified national markings (the crosses on the fuselage and on upper wing surfaces, as well as the swastika and "XR" code letters were not typical white, but dark – grey – green RLM 74).The Balkenkreuz on the port wing undersurface was traditional black with wide white and thin black elements, while the starboard wing, painted black, sported only the white elements of a cross. The beginning of the fuselage code — "G9" — was applied in black in characters four times smaller, which was a general rule for destroyer aircraft in 1943 – 45, and at the end of the war also became common on some bombers.

The most common scheme for night fighters was to paint the aircraft RLM 76 overall and apply on upper (and partly side surfaces) irregular areas or "ribbons" of RLM 75. Heinkel He 219A "Uhus" were painted in this manner as early as mid – 1943, G9+FB, of I./NJG 1 being typical. It carried simplified Balkenkreuze on wings and fuselage, with an identical shape to the cross but applied in black, and not — as on most aircraft — white. Swastikas were also reduced to a black outline. Such simplifica-

tion was typical for the late period of the war (1944/45), but examples can be found of earlier use of such simplified national markings. For example, a Ju 88A–4 of 1./KG 54 used during fighting in Italy, with an unusual camouflage. The scheme was supposed to hide the aircraft over the sea, so upper and side surfaces were painted RLM 75, onto which light grey RLM 76 scribbles or "waves" were applied so as to imitate light reflections from the surface of the sea. Lower surfaces were in RLM 76, also with waves, but these were darker, in RLM 75. Black "EH" code letters were applied next to the dark grey Balkenkreuze which was reduced to an outline, and a band around the rear fuselage, originally white (standard in the Mediterranean theatre), was overpainted

He 111H in typical green camouflage: black – green RLM 70, dark green RLM 71 on upper surfaces and blue RLM 65 on lower ones.

(MVT via M. Krzyżan)

A group of German and Italian airmen during a talk near a three—engined Ju 52/3mg5e in Mediterranean markings — white band around the fuselage. Also partly visible is the code 4Z(?)+I?. The aircraft's upper surfaces were probably painted with RLM 70 only.

(R. Michulec coll.)

(as was the swastika) with dark grey, probably RLM 74.

Grey shades of RLM 74/75/76 were in even wider use, not all of them documented in photographs, although some pictures show to advantage the very interesting scheme of Dornier Do 217J–2, KD+MZ, consisting of RLM 74/75 pattern on wings and tailplane upper surfaces, and fuselage

top. Underside of the entire aircraft and fuselage sides were painted RLM 76, with large irregular areas of RLM 74/75 on sides of the fuselage and engine nacelles, that covered almost the entire side surfaces and left only narrow stripes of the original RLM 76. Crosses on the aircraft were of the 1940 standard with no simplifications.

AFRICAN CAMPAIGN

Large numbers of various camouflage schemes can be observed in photographs portraying aircraft of the African campaign during 1941—43. The previously mentioned LDv 521/2 officially introduced new paint colours for the tropical camouflage — RLM 78/79/80. This took place in November 1941 although the new colours seem to have been in use in the field from the previous August. The new colours would only be definitely applied to new aircraft on assembly lines, while as early as spring 1941 the German air force was involved in fighting with the Allies in the Mediterranean

Messerschmitt Bf 109F–2/trop "white 2" of I./JG 27 shows the desert camouflage of RLM 79 on upper surfaces and RLM 78 on lower. On the engine cowling is the unit emblem — native's head and leopard's head on a map of Africa.

(R. Michulec coll.)

theatre. Where tropical camouflage would have been used, such as implemented by the Italians, Greeks or British, Luftwaffe aircraft wore the standard European temperate "grey" scheme (most often RLM 74/75/76, sometimes RLM 71/02/65 or the green RLM 70/71/65). For example, most Messerschmitt Bf 109 Es of JG 26 and JG 27 wore camouflage of grey tones RLM 74/75/76 — absolutely unsuitable above the desert, where the units would fight. When the Stukas of StG 2 "Immelmann" arrived in the African theatre the only tropical element of the paint scheme was ... the Afrikakorps emblem — a white palm tree with swastika, plus the Luftwaffe eagle — on the engine cowling camouflaged in the "green" RLM 70/71 scheme. For example, Ju 87 B–2 of 4. Staffel, T6+BM, wore such a scheme (it also received a white band around the fuselage following the Italian pattern). According to the German standard the individual letter of the fuselage code was in the Staffel colour — white, as was the propeller spinner tip.

After some time StG 2 dive bombers started to receive desert camouflage in the form of irregular areas of a sand tone, probably the Italian version. The paint was applied rather carelessly — some aircraft had small areas of paint, on others these

A liaison Fi 156 C-3/Trop, DM+BY, in a desert scheme - RLM 70/71 scheme with irregular lines of RLM 79 sand. White fuselage band is a tipical recognition marking on German and Italian aircraft at the Mediterranean Sea.

(R. Michulec coll.)

covered most of the upper and side surfaces. Some aircraft of the unit continued until 1942 without the sand camouflage. Tropical paints: RLM 78, RLM 79 and RLM 80 arrived sooner in the fighter units — for example, some fighters of JG 27 received the desert camouflage during summer. A good example is the Bf 109E–7/trop. "white 12", of 1. Staffel, which had its wing and tail

undersurfaces, as well as lower and side surfaces of the fuselage in the grey blue RLM 78, darker than the "European" RLM 65, or RLM 76, closer to the British Azure Blue. Upper surfaces of the wings, tail and fuselage were painted a light sand — yellow on which irregular areas of olive — brown were applied. The aircraft featured a white band around the rear fuselage, typical for

Some aircraft on arrival to Africa in 1941 were still in "European" camouflage of RLM 70/71/65, sometimes with irregular areas of sand. In the photo Ju 87B–2/Trop, W.Nr. 6117, of StG 2 "Immelmann", ground crew have applied a hasty desert camouflage which obscured part of the code letters on the fuselage.

(P. Jarrett via B. Ketley)

Bf 110D of III./ZG 26 "Horst Wessel Geschwader" flying over the desert, 1942. The division line between RLM 74/75 on upper and RLM 76 on lower surfaces is visible on the fuselage. The tall is painted RLM 76 with dots of RLM 74 and 75 grey applied on it. Above the swastika white symbols of 5 kills are visible.

(P. Jarrett via B. Ketley)

aircraft of the theatre, and a white spinner. It also carried an external fuel tank, not used over Northern France — this was blue like the rest of the aircraft under surfaces (RLM 78). "White 12" did not carry the typical JG 27 yellow nose and rudder, characteristic elements of the earlier period. Not all aircraft were repainted. For example, in July 1941, Staffelkapitän of the Geschwader's 1.Staffel, Oblt. Karl-Wolfgang Redlich, flew Bf 109E–7/Trop. "white 1" in "European" camouflage, RLM 74/75/76 with a yellow nose and rudder, which sported 20 white kill symbols. Camouflage changed, yellow identification markings were replaced with white

ones, but the noses of JG 27's Messerschmitts always proudly displayed the magnificent emblem of the unit, designed a long time earlier, but strangely prophetic in that it anticipated the "African" career of the unit — the badge consisted of a native's head next to a leopard's head, superimposed on a black outline of Africa. Another example of tropical shades introduced by LDv 521/1 was the painting of lower surfaces with RLM 78, while upper — including fuselage sides and vertical tail — were entirely sand RLM 79. This scheme was used on both JG 27 aircraft (for example, "White 6" of 1. Staffel), and in other units,

such as the Bf 109E–7/B/Trop fighter — bomber W.Nr. 6431, S9+IS, of 8./ ZG 1 that attacked British armoured columns in 1942. The plain camouflage sported black code characters „S9+IS", a white band on the fuselage, spinner and wingtips. White fuselage bands and wingtips were standard in 1942, with few exceptions. The uniform RLM 79 camouflage on upper surfaces was also applied to other aircraft types used in Africa, such as the Ju 88, He 111 and Ju 87. In each case the border line between RLM 79 and RLM 78 (i. e. between sand and blue) on the fuselage was always positioned low, at the wing trailing edge. An interesting phenomenon here was raising the line to mid — fuselage so that a straight or wavy line between RLM 79 and RLM 78 was visible on the fuselage side. Such a scheme was factory — applied to Messerschmitt Bf 109s in F ("Friedrich") and G ("Gustav") versions. At that time the darker shade of the sand — brown RLM 79 was used. Factory — fresh aircraft in such camouflage arrived in units in Africa and Italy in 1942 and 1943,

please turn to page 44

Heinkel He 111 H–6 in flight over the Mediterranean in 1944. Fuselage code 1H+EN denotes this machine belonged to 5./KG 26 "Löwen". Red letter "E" and black "N" are clearly visible against the white fuselage band. Near the cockpit — the Geschwader emblem — a red lion in a white shield.

(K. Ries via R. L. Ward)

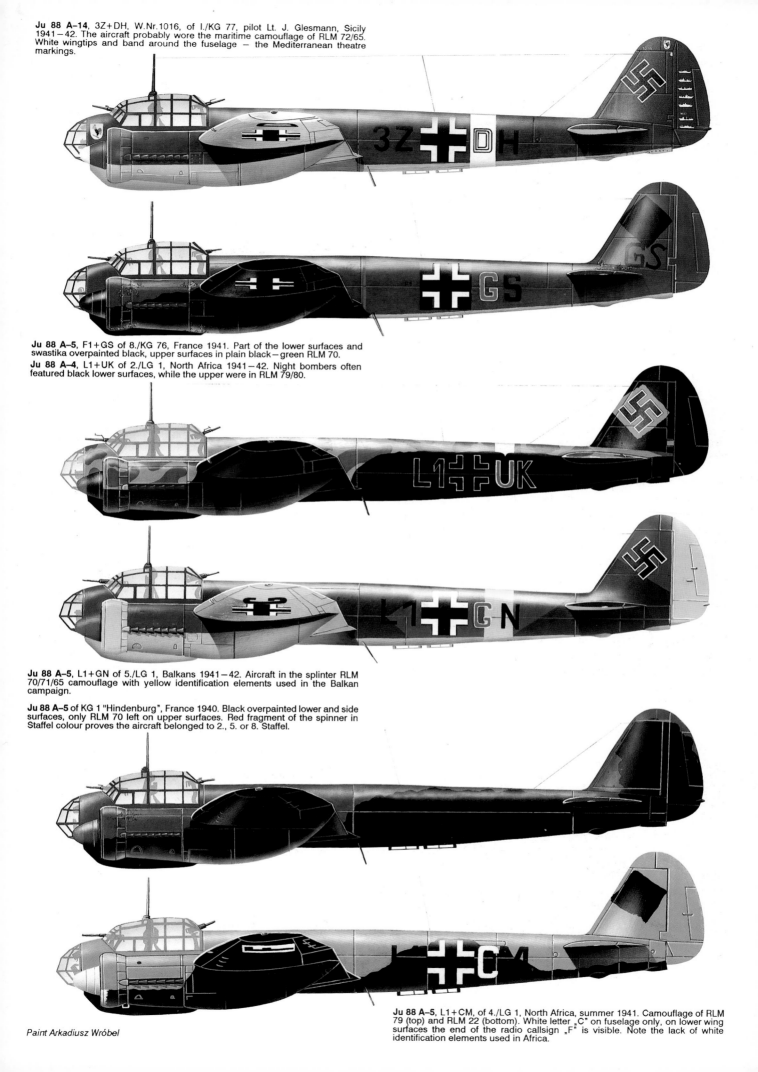

Ju 88 A–14, 3Z+DH, W.Nr.1016, of I./KG 77, pilot Lt. J. Glesmann, Sicily 1941—42. The aircraft probably wore the maritime camouflage of RLM 72/65. White wingtips and band around the fuselage — the Mediterranean theatre markings.

Ju 88 A–5, F1+GS of 8./KG 76, France 1941. Part of the lower surfaces and swastika overpainted black, upper surfaces in plain black—green RLM 70.

Ju 88 A–4, L1+UK of 2./LG 1, North Africa 1941—42. Night bombers often featured black lower surfaces, while the upper were in RLM 79/80.

Ju 88 A–5, L1+GN of 5./LG 1, Balkans 1941—42. Aircraft in the splinter RLM 70/71/65 camouflage with yellow identification elements used in the Balkan campaign.

Ju 88 A–5 of KG 1 "Hindenburg", France 1940. Black overpainted lower and side surfaces, only RLM 70 left on upper surfaces. Red fragment of the spinner in Staffel colour proves the aircraft belonged to 2., 5. or 8. Staffel.

Paint Arkadiusz Wróbel

Ju 88 A–5, L1+CM, of 4./LG 1, North Africa, summer 1941. Camouflage of RLM 79 (top) and RLM 22 (bottom). White letter „C" on fuselage only, on lower wing surfaces the end of the radio callsign „F" is visible. Note the lack of white identification elements used in Africa.

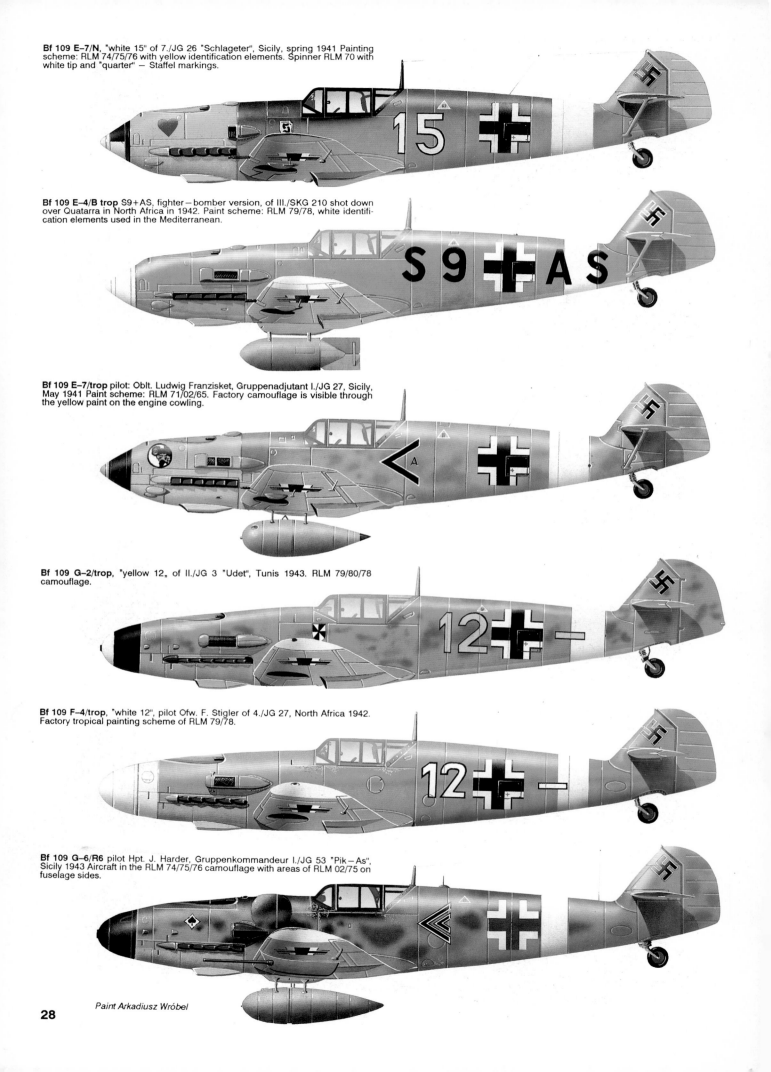

Bf 109 E-7/N, "white 15" of 7./JG 26 "Schlageter", Sicily, spring 1941 Painting scheme: RLM 74/75/76 with yellow identification elements. Spinner RLM 70 with white tip and "quarter" — Staffel markings.

Bf 109 E-4/B trop S9+AS, fighter—bomber version, of III./SKG 210 shot down over Quatarra in North Africa in 1942. Paint scheme: RLM 79/78, white identification elements used in the Mediterranean.

Bf 109 E-7/trop pilot: Oblt. Ludwig Franzisket, Gruppenadjutant I./JG 27, Sicily, May 1941 Paint scheme: RLM 71/02/65. Factory camouflage is visible through the yellow paint on the engine cowling.

Bf 109 G-2/trop, "yellow 12„ of II./JG 3 "Udet", Tunis 1943. RLM 79/80/78 camouflage.

Bf 109 F-4/trop, "white 12", pilot Ofw. F. Stigler of 4./JG 27, North Africa 1942. Factory tropical painting scheme of RLM 79/78.

Bf 109 G-6/R6 pilot Hpt. J. Harder, Gruppenkommandeur I./JG 53 "Pik—As", Sicily 1943 Aircraft in the RLM 74/75/76 camouflage with areas of RLM 02/75 on fuselage sides.

Paint Arkadiusz Wróbel

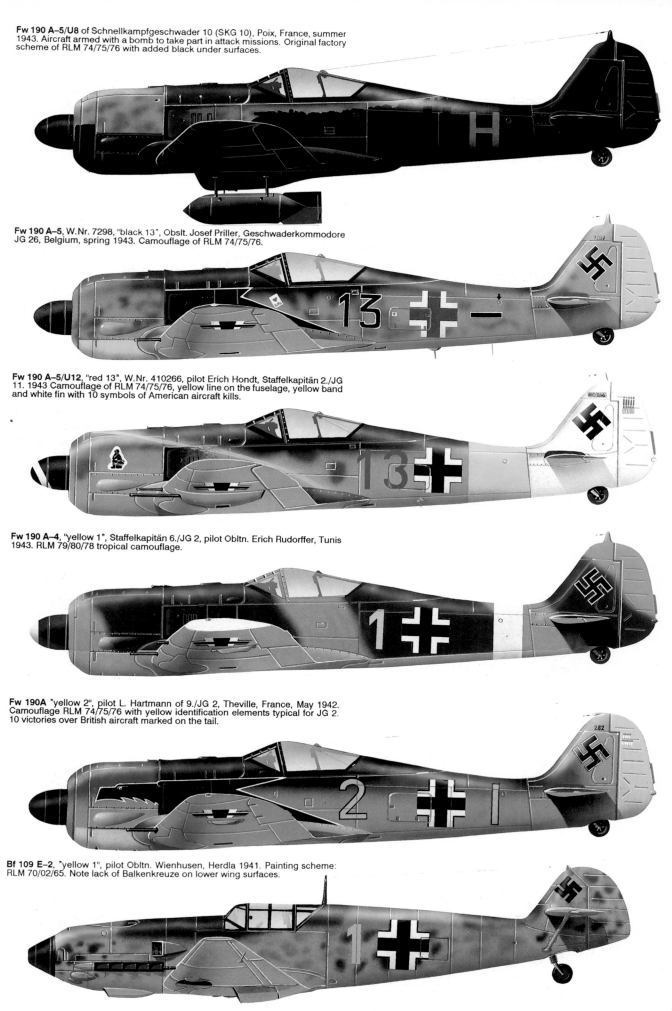

Fw 190 A–5/U8 of Schnellkampfgeschwader 10 (SKG 10), Poix, France, summer 1943. Aircraft armed with a bomb to take part in attack missions. Original factory scheme of RLM 74/75/76 with added black under surfaces.

Fw 190 A–5, W.Nr. 7298, "black 13", Obslt. Josef Priller, Geschwaderkommodore JG 26, Belgium, spring 1943. Camouflage of RLM 74/75/76.

Fw 190 A–5/U12, "red 13", W.Nr. 410266, pilot Erich Hondt, Staffelkapitän 2./JG 11. 1943 Camouflage of RLM 74/75/76, yellow line on the fuselage, yellow band and white fin with 10 symbols of American aircraft kills.

Fw 190 A–4, "yellow 1", Staffelkapitän 6./JG 2, pilot Obltn. Erich Rudorffer, Tunis 1943. RLM 79/80/78 tropical camouflage.

Fw 190A "yellow 2", pilot L. Hartmann of 9./JG 2, Theville, France, May 1942. Camouflage RLM 74/75/76 with yellow identification elements typical for JG 2. 10 victories over British aircraft marked on the tail.

Bf 109 E–2, "yellow 1", pilot Obltn. Wienhusen, Herdla 1941. Painting scheme: RLM 70/02/65. Note lack of Balkenkreuze on lower wing surfaces.

Paint Arkadiusz Wróbel

Ju 88 A–4 of KG 54, Rome (Italy) late 1943. Aircraft with radio callsign PN+MT in the "Wellenmuster" RLM 75/76 camouflage.

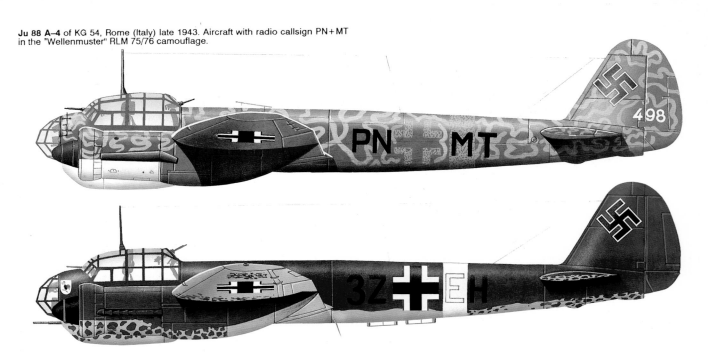

Ju 88 A–14, 3Z+EH, of I./KG 77, Sicily 1942/43. Aircraft armed with a 20mm cannon, used for anti—shipping duties in the Mediterranean, camouflage probably "maritime „ — RLM 72 on upper and RLM 65 on lower surfaces.

Ju 88 A–4, +EH of 1./KG 54 Rome (Italy) 1943. "Wellenmuster" ("Wave Mirror") RLM 75/76 camouflage.

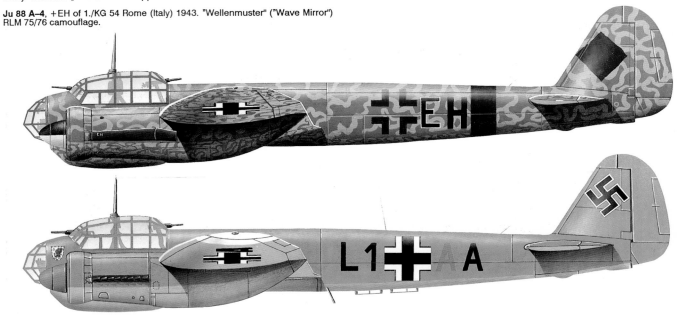

Ju 88 A–5, L1AA of Geschwaderstab LG 1, North Africa 1941—42. Aircraft in tropical camouflage of RLM 79/78. Green spinner and letter "A„ were staff markings.

Do 217 J–2, KD+MZ, 1943, camouflage of RLM 74/75/76.

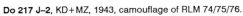

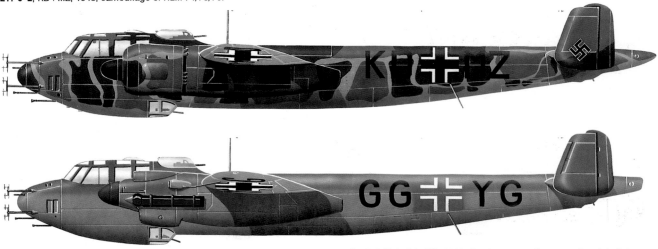

Do 217 N–1, GG+YG, 1943. Another camouflage type for night fighters — RLM 75 on upper and RLM 76 on lower surfaces. Note the lack of swastika.

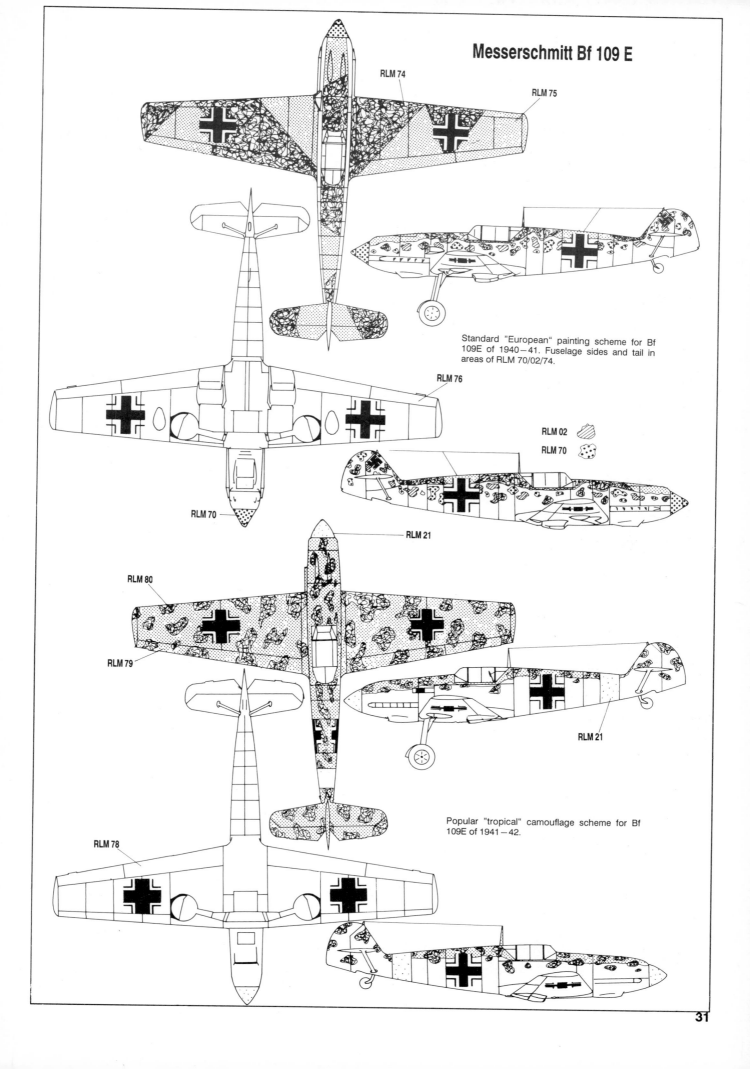

Messerschmitt Bf 109 E

RLM 74

RLM 75

Standard "European" painting scheme for Bf 109E of 1940–41. Fuselage sides and tail in areas of RLM 70/02/74.

RLM 76

RLM 02

RLM 70

RLM 70

RLM 21

RLM 80

RLM 79

RLM 21

RLM 78

Popular "tropical" camouflage scheme for Bf 109E of 1941–42.

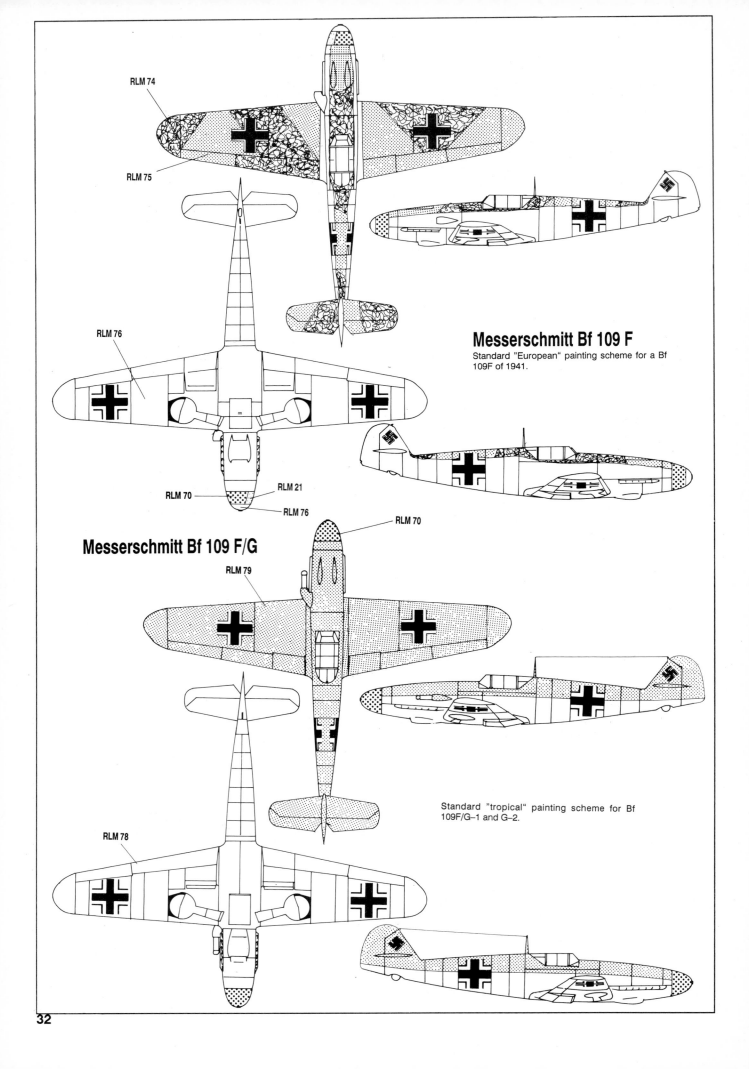

RLM 74

RLM 75

RLM 76

RLM 70　　RLM 21

RLM 76

Messerschmitt Bf 109 F

Standard "European" painting scheme for a Bf 109F of 1941.

RLM 70

RLM 79

Messerschmitt Bf 109 F/G

RLM 78

Standard "tropical" painting scheme for Bf 109F/G–1 and G–2.

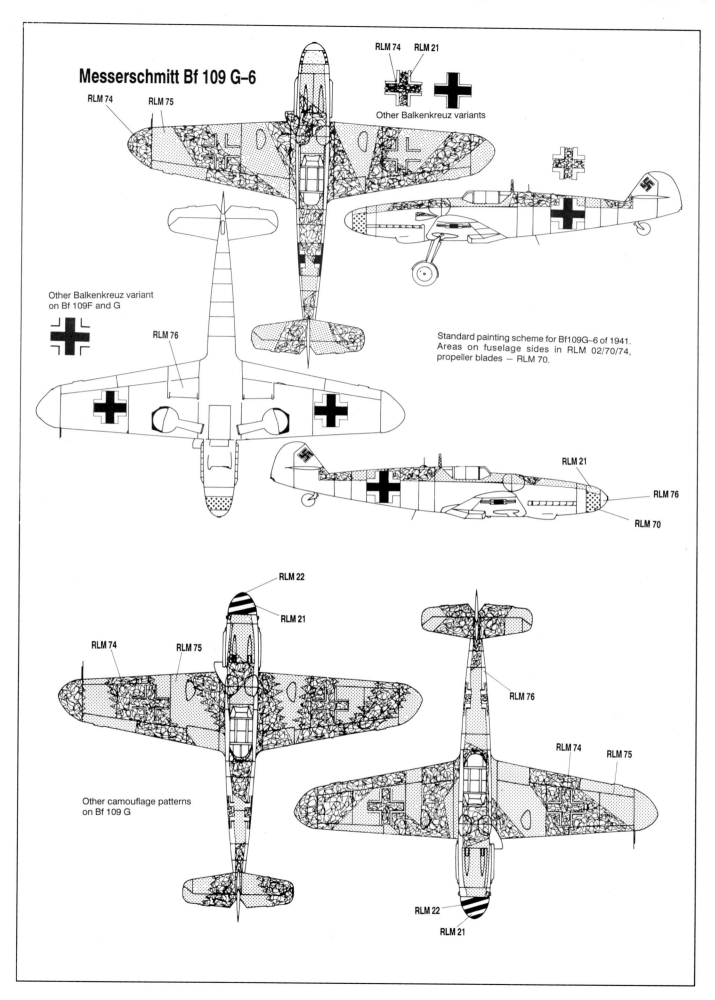

Messerschmitt Bf 109 G-6

RLM 74

RLM 75

RLM 74   RLM 21

Other Balkenkreuz variants

Other Balkenkreuz variant
on Bf 109F and G

RLM 76

Standard painting scheme for Bf109G–6 of 1941.
Areas on fuselage sides in RLM 02/70/74,
propeller blades — RLM 70.

RLM 21

RLM 76

RLM 70

RLM 22

RLM 21

RLM 74

RLM 75

RLM 76

Other camouflage patterns
on Bf 109 G

RLM 74

RLM 75

RLM 22

RLM 21

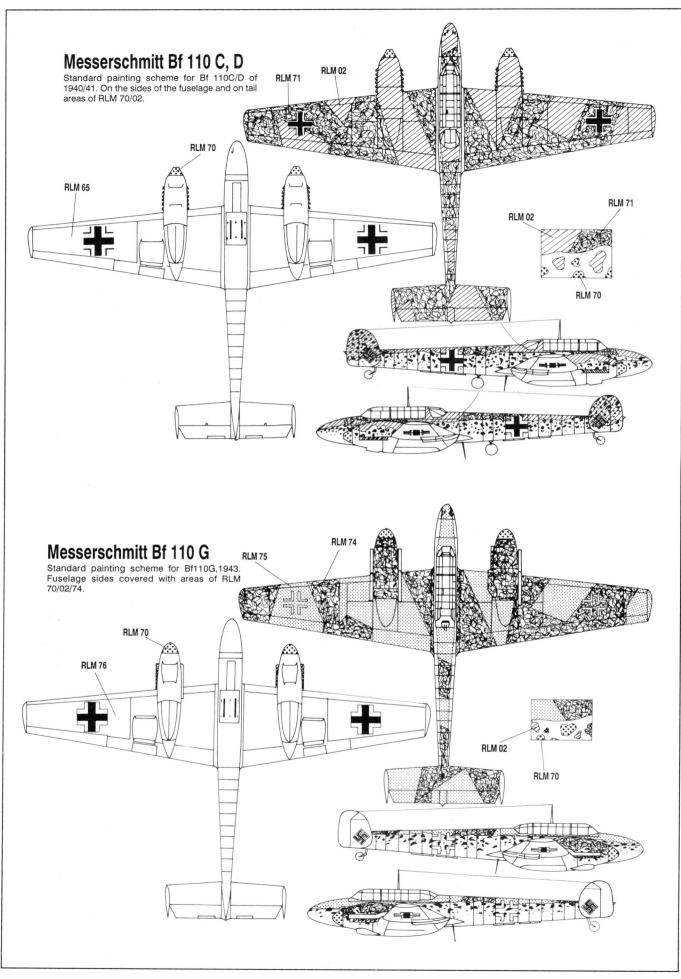

Messerschmitt Bf 110 C, D

Standard painting scheme for Bf 110C/D of 1940/41. On the sides of the fuselage and on tail areas of RLM 70/02.

RLM 71
RLM 02
RLM 70
RLM 65
RLM 02
RLM 71
RLM 70

Messerschmitt Bf 110 G

Standard painting scheme for Bf110G, 1943. Fuselage sides covered with areas of RLM 70/02/74.

RLM 75
RLM 74
RLM 70
RLM 76
RLM 02
RLM 70

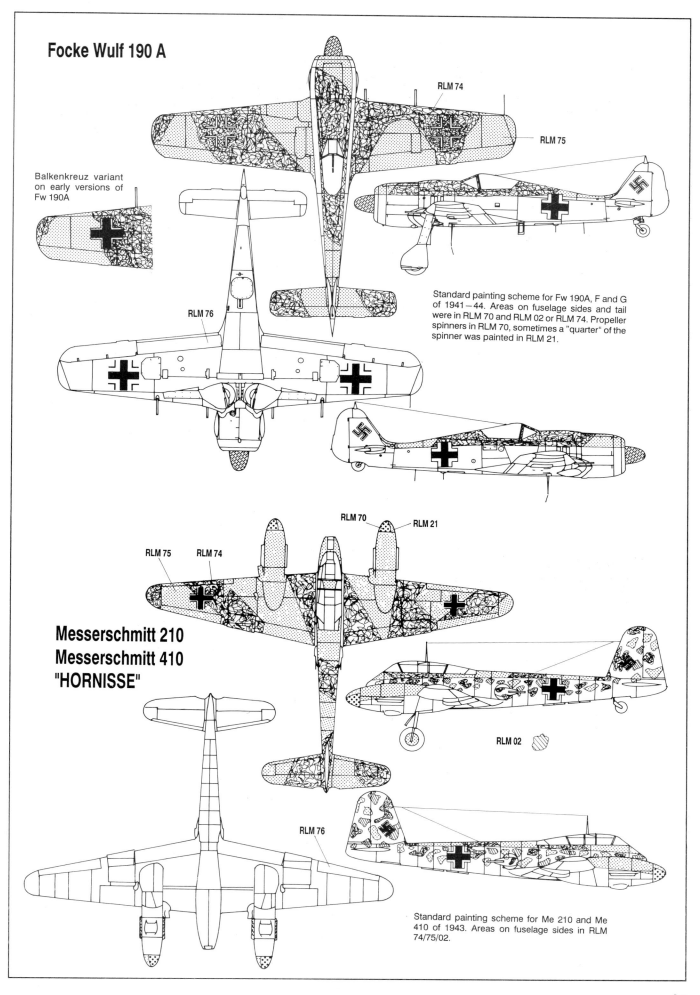

Focke Wulf 190 A

RLM 74

RLM 75

Balkenkreuz variant on early versions of Fw 190A

RLM 76

Standard painting scheme for Fw 190A, F and G of 1941—44. Areas on fuselage sides and tail were in RLM 70 and RLM 02 or RLM 74. Propeller spinners in RLM 70, sometimes a "quarter" of the spinner was painted in RLM 21.

RLM 70   RLM 21

RLM 75   RLM 74

Messerschmitt 210
Messerschmitt 410
"HORNISSE"

RLM 02

RLM 76

Standard painting scheme for Me 210 and Me 410 of 1943. Areas on fuselage sides in RLM 74/75/02.

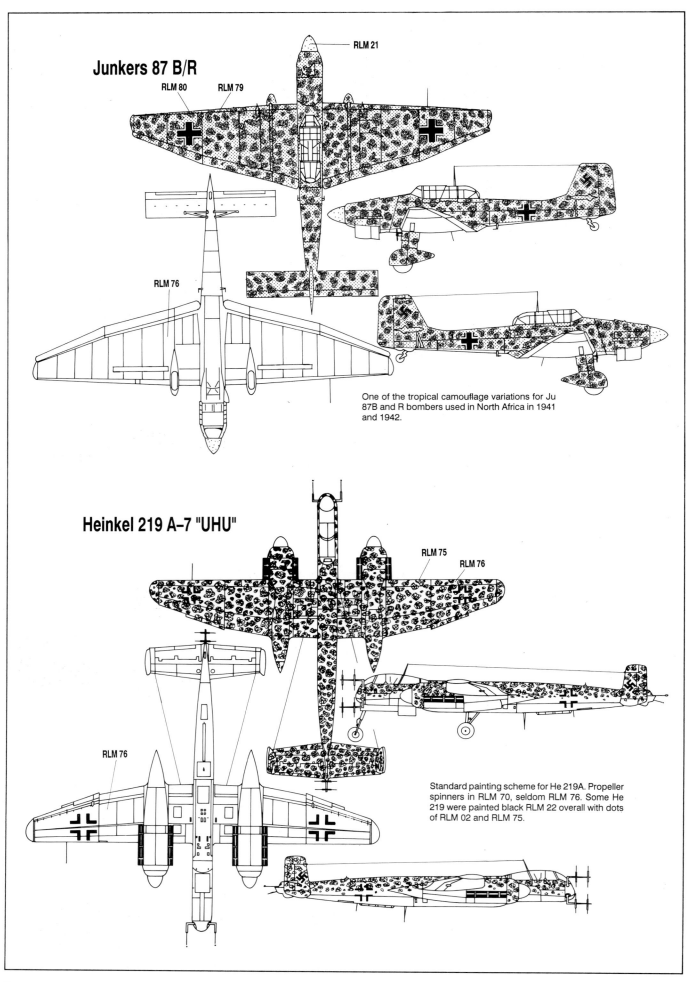

Junkers 87 B/R

RLM 21
RLM 80
RLM 79
RLM 76

One of the tropical camouflage variations for Ju 87B and R bombers used in North Africa in 1941 and 1942.

Heinkel 219 A-7 "UHU"

RLM 75
RLM 76
RLM 76

Standard painting scheme for He 219A. Propeller spinners in RLM 70, seldom RLM 76. Some He 219 were painted black RLM 22 overall with dots of RLM 02 and RLM 75.

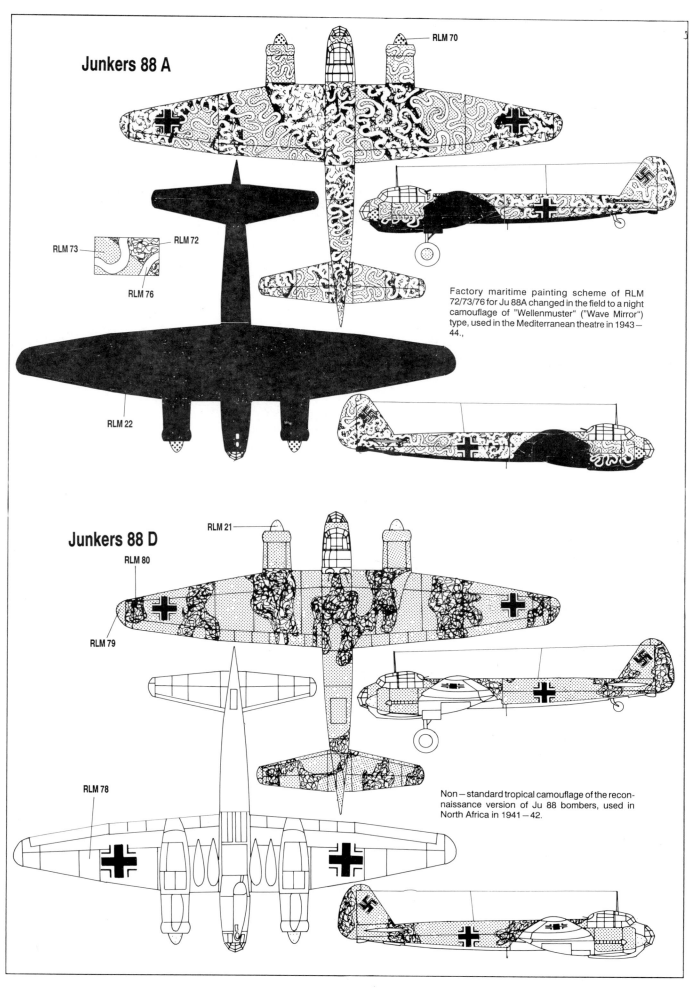

Junkers 88 A

RLM 70

RLM 73 — RLM 72

RLM 76

RLM 22

Factory maritime painting scheme of RLM 72/73/76 for Ju 88A changed in the field to a night camouflage of "Wellenmuster" ("Wave Mirror") type, used in the Mediterranean theatre in 1943—44.,

Junkers 88 D

RLM 21

RLM 80

RLM 79

RLM 78

Non—standard tropical camouflage of the reconnaissance version of Ju 88 bombers, used in North Africa in 1941—42.

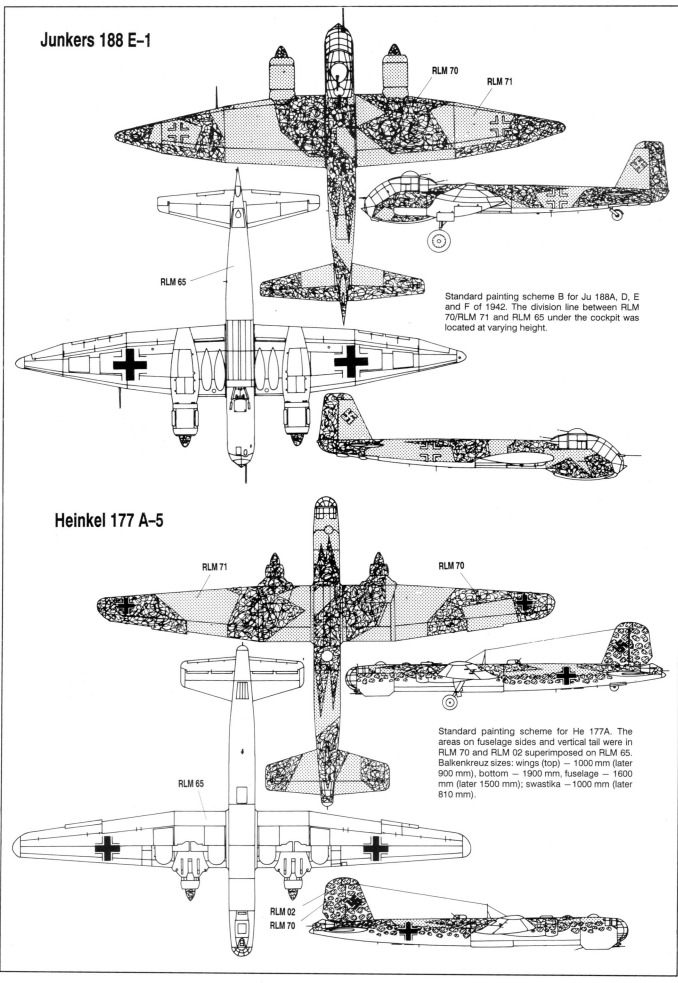

Junkers 188 E-1

RLM 70
RLM 71
RLM 65

Standard painting scheme B for Ju 188A, D, E and F of 1942. The division line between RLM 70/RLM 71 and RLM 65 under the cockpit was located at varying height.

Heinkel 177 A-5

RLM 71
RLM 70
RLM 65
RLM 02
RLM 70

Standard painting scheme for He 177A. The areas on fuselage sides and vertical tail were in RLM 70 and RLM 02 superimposed on RLM 65. Balkenkreuz sizes: wings (top) — 1000 mm (later 900 mm), bottom — 1900 mm, fuselage — 1600 mm (later 1500 mm); swastika — 1000 mm (later 810 mm).

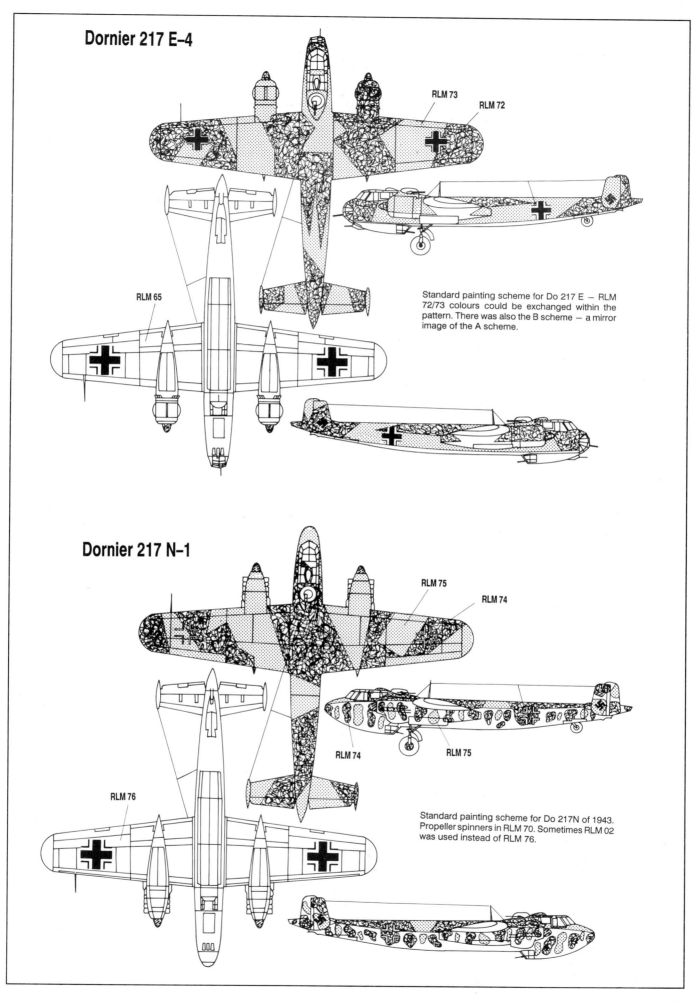

Dornier 217 E–4

RLM 73

RLM 72

RLM 65

Standard painting scheme for Do 217 E — RLM 72/73 colours could be exchanged within the pattern. There was also the B scheme — a mirror image of the A scheme.

Dornier 217 N–1

RLM 75

RLM 74

RLM 74

RLM 75

RLM 76

Standard painting scheme for Do 217N of 1943. Propeller spinners in RLM 70. Sometimes RLM 02 was used instead of RLM 76.

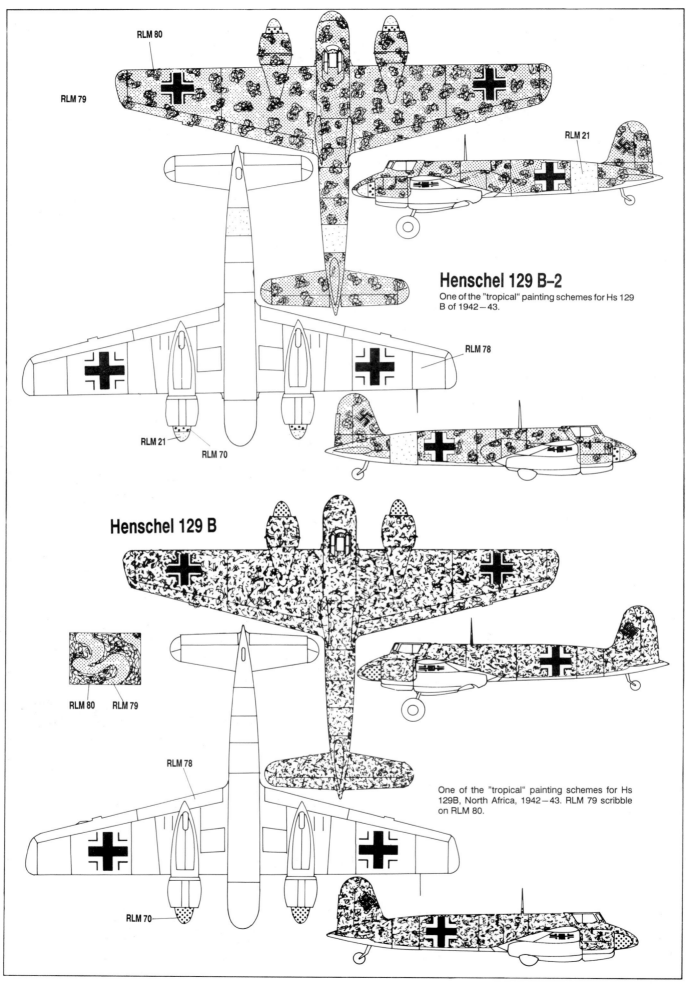

RLM 80

RLM 79

RLM 21

Henschel 129 B-2

One of the "tropical" painting schemes for Hs 129 B of 1942—43.

RLM 78

RLM 21

RLM 70

Henschel 129 B

RLM 80   RLM 79

RLM 78

One of the "tropical" painting schemes for Hs 129B, North Africa, 1942—43. RLM 79 scribble on RLM 80.

RLM 70

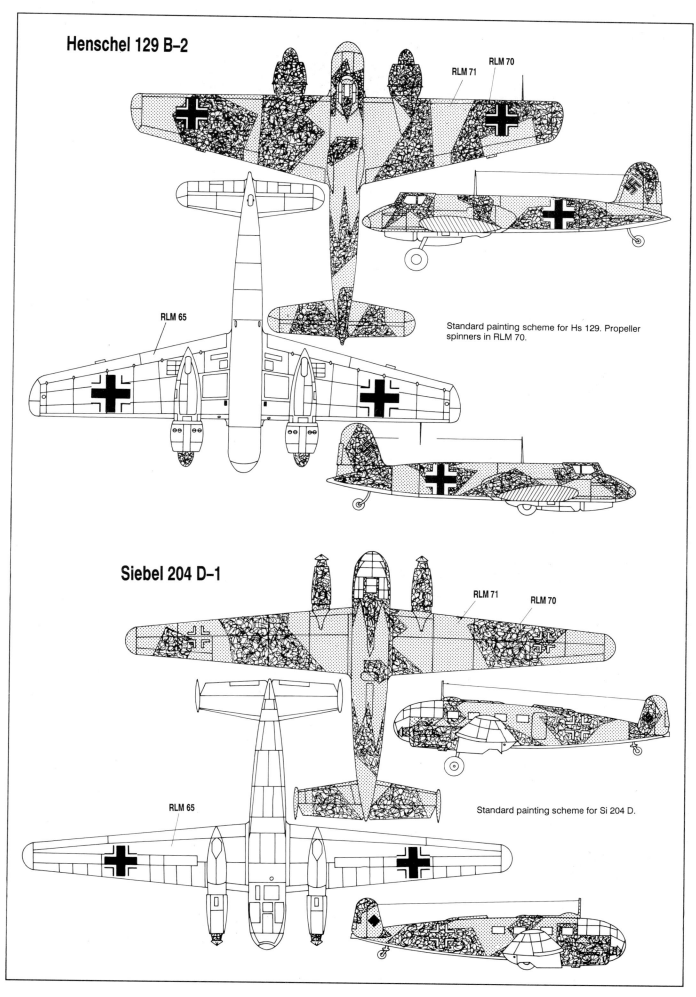

Henschel 129 B-2

RLM 71
RLM 70

RLM 65

Standard painting scheme for Hs 129. Propeller spinners in RLM 70.

Siebel 204 D-1

RLM 71
RLM 70

RLM 65

Standard painting scheme for Si 204 D.

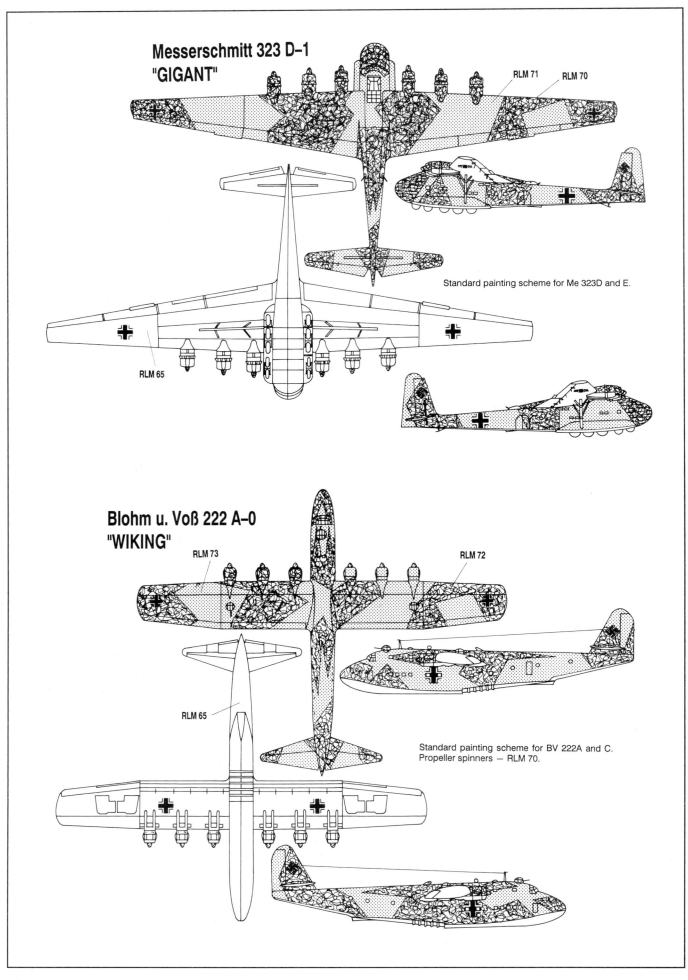

Messerschmitt 323 D–1 "GIGANT"

RLM 71 RLM 70

RLM 65

Standard painting scheme for Me 323D and E.

Blohm u. Voß 222 A–0 "WIKING"

RLM 73 RLM 72

RLM 65

Standard painting scheme for BV 222A and C.
Propeller spinners — RLM 70.

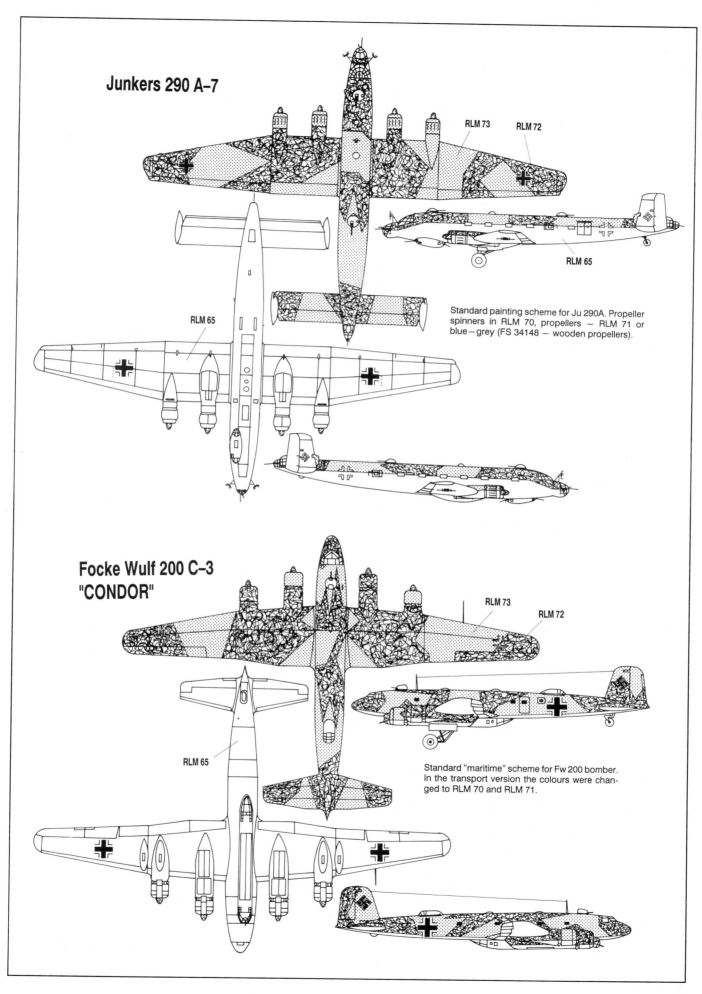

Junkers 290 A-7

RLM 73
RLM 72
RLM 65
RLM 65

Standard painting scheme for Ju 290A. Propeller spinners in RLM 70, propellers — RLM 71 or blue–grey (FS 34148 — wooden propellers).

Focke Wulf 200 C-3 "CONDOR"

RLM 73
RLM 72
RLM 65

Standard "maritime" scheme for Fw 200 bomber. In the transport version the colours were changed to RLM 70 and RLM 71.

USUAL POSITIONS OF LUFTWAFFE UNIT EMBLEMS IN 1940–43.

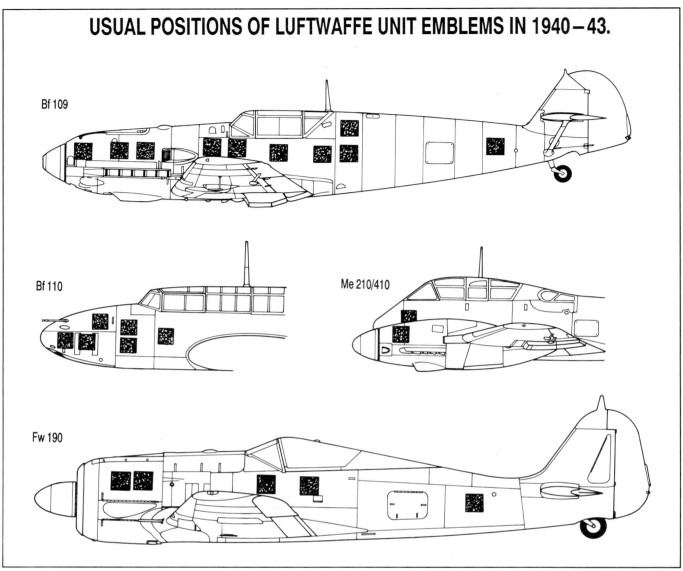

Bf 109

Bf 110

Me 210/410

Fw 190

from page 26

and even — according to some sources — the Eastern Front. Additional irregular areas of olive—green RLM 80 were applied at front—line maintenance units. The size of these varied — from fist—size blotches, for example, on the Bf 109G–2/Trop. "black 1" of 5. Staffel/JG 53, up to large segments, as on Bf 109G–2/Trop. "white 2" of 7. Staffel of the same Geschwader. Aircraft of the unit featured very interesting camouflage and markings. For example, white wingtips were rare on „Pik—As" Messerschmitts. It was on JG 53 Bf 109Fs and Gs that RLM 80 olive—green areas were applied, while other units did that very seldom — both JG 3's and JG 27's "Friedrichs" and "Gustavs" flew in the single—tone camouflage on upper surfaces.

An extremely interesting example of camouflage is provided by the previously mentioned scheme on the Bf 109G–2/Trop. "black 1" of 5./JG 53, based in Sicily in October 1942. Top of the fuselage down to mid—height of the sides, complete with the fin, was covered with tiny dots of olive—green RLM 80 and sand—brown RLM 79. Lower portion of the fuselage, wing and tail

A pair of Messerschmitt Bf 110 Cs of ZG 26 over the Mediterranean, Spring 1941. Both aircraft are painted in a shade of sand (probably with an Italian paint), black codes, emblem on the nose and a white band around the fuselage (elements typical for the theatre).

(MVT via M. Krzyżan)

EXAMPLES OF VICTORY MARKINGS ON FIGHTER AIRCRAFT TAILS IN LUFTWAFFE 1940–43

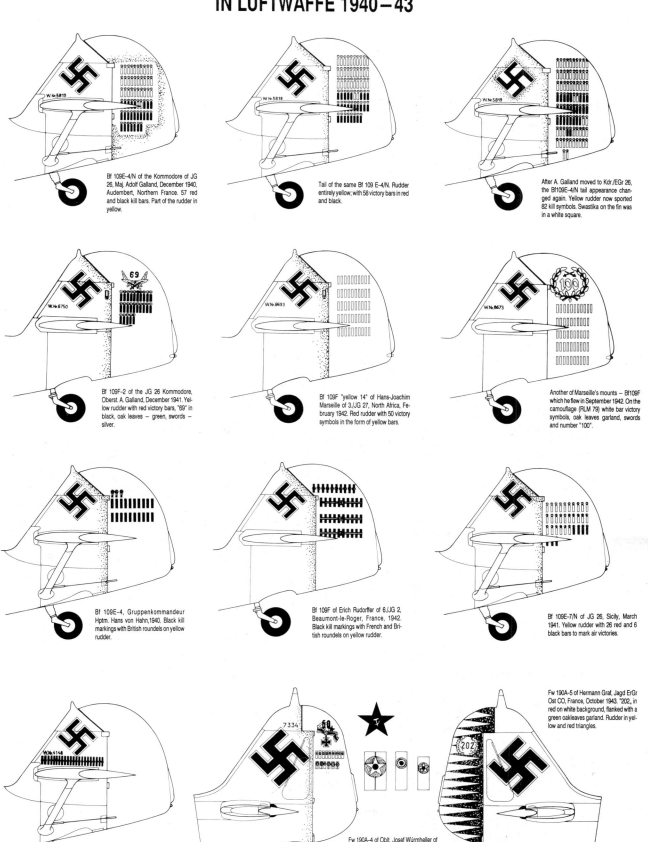

Bf 109E-4/N of the Kommodore of JG 26, Maj. Adolf Galland, December 1940, Audembert, Northern France. 57 red and black kill bars. Part of the rudder in yellow.

Tail of the same Bf 109 E-4/N. Rudder entirely yellow; with 58 victory bars in red and black.

After A. Galland moved to Kdr./EGr 26, the Bf109E-4/N tail appearance changed again. Yellow rudder now sported 82 kill symbols. Swastika on the fin was in a white square.

Bf 109F-2 of the JG 26 Kommodore, Oberst. A. Galland, December 1941. Yellow rudder with red victory bars, "69" in black, oak leaves – green, swords – silver.

Bf 109F "yellow 14" of Hans-Joachim Marseille of 3./JG 27, North Africa, February 1942. Red rudder with 50 victory symbols in the form of yellow bars.

Another of Marseille's mounts – Bf109F which he flew in September 1942. On the camouflage (RLM 79) white bar victory symbols, oak leaves garland, swords and number "100".

Bf 109E-4, Gruppenkommandeur Hptm. Hans von Hahn, 1940. Black kill markings with British roundels on yellow rudder.

Bf 109F of Erich Rudorffer of 6./JG 2, Beaumont-le-Roger, France, 1942. Black kill markings with French and British roundels on yellow rudder.

Bf 109E-7/N of JG 26, Sicily, March 1941. Yellow rudder with 26 red and 6 black bars to mark air victories.

Bf 109E-7, Kommandeur II./JG 27, Balkans, April 1941. On the camouflage (RLM 74/75/76) black bars with British roundels.

Fw 190A-4 of Oblt. Josef Würmheller of II./JG 2, France, 1943. Yellow rudder sports Ritterkreuz zum Eichenlaub, on a British roundel and Soviet star. Below white bars with British roundels and American stars ("double" denote bombers shot down).

Fw 190A-5 of Hermann Graf, Jagd ErGr Ost CO, France, October 1943. "202" in red on white background, flanked with a green oakleaves garland. Rudder in yellow and red triangles.

undersurfaces were blue (RLM 78). Rudder, however, was in the old „European " camouflage of blue – grey background (RLM 76) with small areas of RLM 74/02/70. The difference in colours testifies that the original rudder was damaged and replaced with another. This could have been removed from an earlier Bf 109 variant (for example, E or F), which flew in Africa with the old camouflage of RLM 74/75/76. In general, the fighters destined for the Mediterranean received the factory camouflage of RLM 79/78, but some aircraft reached Africa straight from other theatres, for example from the West or Russia. These aircraft arrived over the desert in "grey" schemes, often with characteristic markings, for example yellow noses (JG 53). These elements were overpainted or reduced and, in residual form, continued through the years of war.

Below: A unique photograph of a He 111 in desert camouflage of RLM 79 on upper surfaces which also shows a portion of the earlier "green" camouflage of RLM 70/71 (in the place where a wing – fuselage fillet has been removed). The emblem below the glazing is also interesting; it was seen on KG 54 aircraft; for example Ju 87s and Bf 110s.

(R. L. Ward)

ITALIAN FRONT

When in 1943 the African front became — thanks to the Allied advances — the Italian front, Messerschmitt 109s of the G–6 variant started to arrive in the RLM 74/75/76 „grey" camouflage scheme again, and were not repainted in tropical shades. An example is provided by the Bf 109 G–6 "black 16" of 5. Staffel JG 53 „Pik – As" with the "Ace of Spades" emblem on the engine cowling, which was painted in a standard scheme of RLM 74/75/76 with fuselage sides and vertical tail covered in areas of RLM 74/70/02. Traditionally for the Mediterranean, a white band was carried around the fuselage. A typical recognition marking for the unit's aircraft was yellow on part of the engine cowlings. Crosses on upper wing surface were reduced to white, while the fuselage ones only lost their thin black outline.

A scrapyard of German aircraft in North Africa. In the foreground — wings of a Bf 109 with white tips seen to advantage and large Balkenkreuze on lower surfaces. In the background, a Bf 110, 3U+DJ, of III./ZG 26 in "European" camouflage of RLM 74/75/76 with white band around the fuselage and a yellow individual letter "D". Far back a wrecked Bf 109E in "desert" painting of RLM 78/80/79.

(R. Michulec coll.

NON-STANDARD UNIT EMBLEMS ON BF 110
(1940-43)

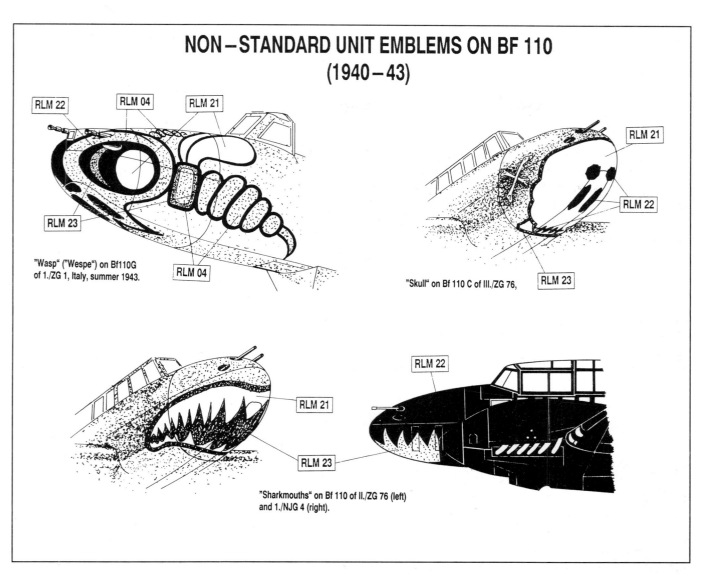

"Wasp" ("Wespe") on Bf110G
of 1./ZG 1, Italy, summer 1943.

"Skull" on Bf 110 C of III./ZG 76,

"Sharkmouths" on Bf 110 of II./ZG 76 (left)
and 1./NJG 4 (right).

"SHARKMOUTH" ON Bf 109

"Sharkmouth" on a Bf 109C-1 of 2./JG 71.

"Tante Ju" — Ju 52/3m, NJ+NH of Minensuchgruppe 1 fitted with electromagnetic ring for minesweeping, flies over the Mediterranean. The RLM 72/73 camouflage scheme is clearly visible on the wings. White band around the fuselage and white tips of wings undersurface were typical on Luftwaffe aircraft in this area.

(P. Jarrett via B. Ketley)

Balkenkreuze on lower wing surfaces and swastika were left unchanged, in traditional form. "Black 16" was outlined in white, as was the vertical bar denoting III. Gruppe. The spinner sported a black-white spiral of four curves, which was becoming increasingly widespread in 1943 on fighters and close support aircraft.

Fw 190 A fighters, similar to Bf 109s, were painted both in the tropical RLM 78/79/80 scheme, and in the European one

Above: One of the "desert" camouflage types was made up of olive (RLM 80) segments on a sand background (RLM 79). This scheme was applied to attack Hs 129 B–2s of 8./SchG 2 at Tripoli in 1942. Blue letter "O", with a white chevron denoting commander (like in fighter units); on the aerial mast is a C.O. pennant. White band around the fuselage and white wingtips typical for the Mediterranean theatre.

(R. Michulec coll.)

Below: Junkers 88 of KG 54 "Totenkopfgeschwader" camouflaged with nets. Under the cockpit is the Geschwader "death's head" emblem ("Totenkopf").

(R. Michulec coll.)

of RLM 74/75/76. In 1942 JG 2 was equipped with Focke—Wulfs that wore both camouflage types. Similar was the case of other typical aircraft — some wore desert, some European camouflage, which for example in the case of the Bf 110 meant RLM 74/75/76, and in the case of other aircraft, such as the Ju 88, He 111 or Hs 129 — a scheme of RLM 70/71/65 or RLM 70/65 greens. Sometimes both schemes were united and irregular areas of scribbles of sand—yellow RLM 79 were applied on standard European camouflage. Scribbles were often applied to Henschel Hs 129s, liaison Fi 156 Storchs, Fw 58 and reconnaissance Henschel Hs 126s. Interesting schemes were applied to Junkers Ju 88s — their camouflage schemes included practically every shade of paint used in the Luftwaffe in 1940/43. The main scheme for bomber aircraft of the period consisted of upper surfaces in black—green (RLM 70) and dark—green (RLM 71), while under surfaces were blue—grey RLM 65. However, some Ju 88s — for example of KG 77 — operating in 1941 over the Mediterranean had their upper surfaces in uniform RLM 70 finish. In 1941 night operations were carried out by Ju 88A–5 aircraft of KG 76, which attacked targets in Britain. These were camouflaged black on their lower surfaces, for protection from the British searchlights. Often the black was carried up the fuselage sides, so that the white markings and code letters did not stand out against the night camouflage. Only the red

Below: Clearly visible pattern of the camouflage colours on an Me 210A — on the wings, tailplane and fuselage top splinter areas of RLM 74/75, on fuselage sides and on the vertical tail areas of RLM 02/70/74.

(MAP)

Right: Bf 109 G-5 ,"white 2", of 7./JG 27, Mediterranean, 1943. standard "grey" camouflage of RLM 74/75/76, white markings of this area: fuselage band and rudder. Blackgreen (RLM 70) spinner with white "quarter". Balkenkreuz without any thin black outline typical for the 1943-1945 period.

(P. Jarrett via B. Ketley)

Below right: Wrecked Junkers Ju 88 in the "Wellenmuster" ("Wave Mirror") camouflage used on KG 54 bombers in the Rome area in 1943. On the maritime camouflage of RLM 73/72 brighter wavy lines of RLM 76 or RLM 65.

(R. Michulec coll.)

elements (spinners and code letters) were left unchanged, since in poor lighting red is almost black, and remains poorly visible even when in a searchlight beam. Similarly on British bombers wearing black camouflage, red codes were standard.

Tropical Ju 88 schemes in 1941 and 1942 were encountered in several variations; the first was a finish of sand RLM 79 on the entire upper surfaces, with lower ones in blue RLM 78 (for example, Ju 88A–5, L1+AA, of LG 1 Stab). This scheme was developed into one in which RLM 78 on lower surfaces was replaced with black to camouflage the bomber at night (for example, Ju 88A–5, L1+CM, of 4./LG 1). Another variant was obtained by applying, with a brush or spraygun, irregular areas of olive–green RLM 80 on sand RLM 79 upper surfaces, while lower surfaces were left in blue RLM 78 (for example, Ju 87D–4,7A+GH, of 1.(F)/121) or black (for example, Ju 88 A–4, L1+UK, of 2./LG 1).

"Wellenmuster" – "Wave Mirror" – was the name of another scheme, used on Junkers acting above the Mediterranean sea against enemy shipping. This consisted of standard maritime camouflage RLM 72/73/65 with superimposed wavy lines of RLM 76 on the upper surfaces, supposed to resemble light reflections on sea waves. A variation of the scheme was obtained by using standard fighter and destroyer paints, i.e. RLM 75/76. Aircraft painted overall with the grey–mauve RLM 75 received a

Above right: At the end of 1942 experiments with "night" camouflage were carried on bombers. The Dornier Do 217 E-2 of KG 6 in the photo is RLM 22 black on the undersides while the upper sides are in standard "martime" pattern with thin lines of RLM 76 grey to imitate moonlight reflections on the water. White code letter painted on the cockpit framing.

(P. Jarrett via B. Ketley)

Right: Bf 109 F-4/B with a bomb under the fuselage, used as a fighter-bomber in the Western Front (1941-1942). White bomb shape between the fuselage cross and the tall was a Jabo Staffel marking.

(P. Jarrett via B. Ketley)

**Above: Fw 190 A-3 of 7./JG 2 "Richthofen",
Northern France 1942. All the aircraft are in
"grey" camouflage of RLM 74/75/76. The fighter
nearest camera has the 7. Staffel emblem on
the cowling a black hand with a top-hat on a
white disc. "White 8" and a vertical bar - the
emblem of III.Gruppe.**
(P. Jarrett via B. Ketley)

**Right: Fw 190A of IV/JG 1 in "grey" RLM
74/75/76 camouflage, summer 1942. Par-
ticularly rare IV Gruppe marking - a circle on
the fuselage, behind the Balkenkreuz. Unit
emblem is visible on the cowling.**
(MVT via M. Krzyżan)

grid of waves in blue—grey RLM 76 (for
example, Ju 88A–6/U, radio call sign
PN+MT, W.Nr. 4198, of KG 54). Another
example is provided by fighter Ju 88C–6s
used in night fighter units, painted overall
RLM 76 with upper surfaces embellished in
dots of RLM 75 and RLM 70 (for example,
Ju 88C–6, 4R+AS, of 8./NJG 2, 1943) or
large areas of RLM 75 (for example, Ju
88C–6, R4+FM, of II./NJG 2, 1942) So,
since the Junkers Ju 88 was a multi—role
machine and was used on all fronts, it en-
joyed a wide range of painting schemes and
markings.

**Dornier Do 217E in a "green" camouflage with
"martime shades" RLM 72/73/65. At the centre
of the fuselage Balkankreuz, and under the
cockpit, a white 36 is visible. The wing crosses
have non-standard proportions (wider white
elements).**
(P. Jarrett via B. Ketley)

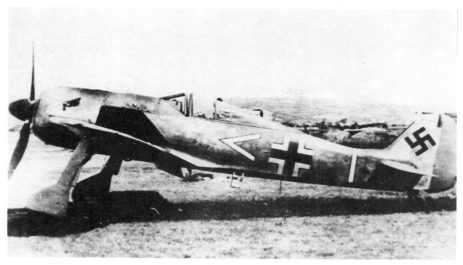

An Fw 190 A-3 of Oblt. Arnim Faber, adjutant of III./JG 2 "Richthofen" in 1942. RLM 74/75/76 camouflage, loower portion of engine cowling red, rudder yellow, black panel behind the engine cowling. The chevron next to Balkenkreuz is an adjutant marking. The III gruppe emblem (cock head) was apllied to both sides of the cowling.

(MVT via M. Krzyżan)

NON–STANDARD NOSES ON LUF-TWAFFE AIRCRAFT

Apart from the quick recognition elements used from mid–1940, such as yellow or white fuselage noses, tails or wingtips, aircraft also carried unit badges and personal emblems, award symbols (for example, Ritterkreuzes), kill markings etc.

An interesting motif was the sharkmouth in red with white teeth applied to the fuselage noses of ZG 76 Messerschmitt Bf 110s as the unit emblem. Such an "American" motif would seem improbable in the Luftwaffe, and yet, in 1940 Zerstörers fought over Dunkirk with sharkmouths, just as the P–40s did in China later on. One example is the Bf 110C–2, M8+EP, of 6. Staffel painted in the RLM 70/71/65 scheme with yellow "E" on the fuselage and wing upper surfaces next to the Balkenkreuz (yellow – the Staffel colour – was also used on spinner tips). The sharkmouth was applied to the lower forward fuselage around the mg/cannon compartment. In 1941, a new camouflage scheme was introduced – the RLM 74/75/76, but the sharkmouths on the forward fuselage continued to feature as the non–standard Geschwader emblem. Inevitably, there were exceptions to the rule; in III. Gruppe a "skull" was applied instead of the sharkmouth, with "eyes" around the gun ports in the nose. The white skull was accompanied by crossed bones on the side panels of the machine gun compartment. Another example of an interesting marking taking the form of large artwork was the symbol of ZG 1 – a large – headed wasp on the forward fuselage of Bf 110 Cs, Fs and Gs, stretching from the nose back to the windscreen (in Italy in 1943 and also on the Eastern Front). A Bf 110G–2/Trop., 2J+CN, of 5. Staffel based in Italy in 1943 sported the units name – symbol – a wasp ("Wespen" was the Geschwader's nickname in German). Camouflage of the aircraft consisted of typical fighter and destroyer (Bf 110) colours – RLM 74/75/76. White band on the fuselage was a Mediterranean theatre marking. The begin-

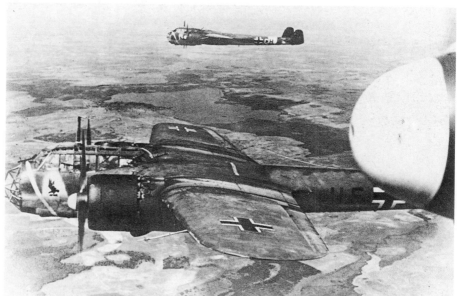

Dornier over Greece in 1941 - Do 17 Z-2s of I./KG 2 "Holzhammer", see how the Balkenkreuzes are positioned. U5 on the fuselage in KG 2 code, the aircraft in the background sports white individual letter "C", while on the white band around the fuselage a black letter "H" - the code of 1. Staffel.

Yellow 5 of Hptm. Erbo von Kaganeck (Bf 109 E) taxiing after landing at a Sicily airfield, Spring 1941. The Messerschmitt has "European" camouflage of RLM 74/75/76, white band around the fuselage, yellow rudder with 14 black bars (kills), forward fuselage with exception of the circle around the yellow 5, which has a black outline, propeller spinner in yellow and RLM 70 blackgreen striping.

(both P. Jarrett via B. Ketley)

A group of Bf 110 D-3 Zerstörers of 4./ZG 76 at a Greek airfield in 1941. The sharkmouth motif was a quick identification marking for the unit's aircraft. The underwing drop tanks were partly painted RLM 71.

(MVT via M. Krzyżan)

ning of the code — 2N — was four times smaller than standard, the individual letter was in standard size and was painted in the Staffel colour (red), as were the spinner tips. Crosses were black without black outline.

Eagles were a popular heraldic motif, used in many Luftwaffe unit emblems, but JG 2 used it in a previously unseen form. In 1942, after re-arming the unit with Fw 190As, a large stylised eagle head began to be applied on fuselage sides (close to the engine collector exhaust) in black with a white outline, which covered large portions of engine cowling and as far back as the wing trailing edge. Focke — Wulfs wore the RLM 74/75/76 camouflage at that time, with yellow or red quick identification markings — rudder and lower engine cowlings. The eagle head on individual examples differed slightly, for example, Fw 190A–3, W.Nr. 2387, "black 11" of 8. Staffel carried the head with a simplified shape of the beak. Other aircraft, for example the Fw 190A–4, W.Nr. 0514, "yellow 2", of 9. Staffel had a headless eagle — after the movable part of the engine cowling was replaced with one that lacked the emblem.

AIRCRAFT MARKINGS IN THE WEST

After the Battle of Britain was lost, the German air force also lost the initiative in the West, and in 1942 — after the British and American forces united in mounting a powerful air offensive against targets in the Reich — the Germans found themselves on the defensive. In that period fighter aircraft based in Northern France and used to intercept Allied bomber formations still carried quick identification elements in the form of yellow, red or white rudders and engine cowlings, inherited from the Battle of Britain. Even though the equipment changed (Bf 109Es were replaced with more modern Bf 109Fs and Gs as well as Fw 190As), still the aircraft of, for example, JG 26 or JG 2 sported yellow identification markings. Most commonly these covered the entire fuselage noses and rudders or just parts of these. For example, Focke — Wulf Fw 190As in JG 26 had only the lower engine cowlings and rudders in yellow — Fw

Fiesler Fi 156 in flight, presents the "martime" camouflage of RLM 73/72/65. The individual colour areas and Balkenkreuzes positioning is well visible.

(P. Jarrett via B. Ketley)

Blohm und Voss Bv 138 flying boat, like all Luftwaffe seaplanes, wore the "maritime" camouflage of RLM 73/72/65. Spinner and blades of the propeller were black green RLM 70.

(R. Michulec coll.)

190A–2, W.Nr. 269, "black 1" of II. Gruppe (camouflage RLM 74/75/76). Yellow (RLM 04) also appeared on Messerschmitt Bf 109s — in April 1941 Adolf Galland, a fighter ace in command of JG 26, flew the Bf 109F–2, W.Nr. 6714, with a yellow nose, including the spinner, and a yellow rudder on which 58 red and 2 black kill markings were applied by the ground crew. Grey camouflage in RLM 74/75/76 was completed by the Commanders bars and chevrons in black with white outlines, and the Geschwader emblem under the cockpit on both fuselage sides. In 1943 rear fuselage bands began to appear in the West. These served to identify units. Later, during 1944, a more sophisticated system of standard colour bands was developed; the so called "Reichsverteidigung Band" — "Reich Defence bands". In the second half of 1943 Fw 190s of JG 1 "Oesau" used red on lower portions of the engine cowling and rudder. The use of red fuselage bands became more frequent. Later still, the red band became the JG 300 emblem.

In JGr 50, under Eastern Front hero, Maj. Hermann Graf, white was used as the Gruppe identification colour among the German defence formations. White was applied to the rudder alone or even the entire vertical surfaces, such as the Bf 109 G–6/R6 flown by the Gruppenkommandeur himself — W.Nr. 15919, "red 1", was in standard RLM 74/75/76 scheme with 105 kill markings on the all-white tail.

MARITIME CAMOUFLAGE

RLM 72/73/65 colours were used on aircraft that attacking Allied convoys in the Atlantic in 1941—44. These activities were controlled by the Fliegerführer Atlantik (Atlantic Command) created in March 1941. Maritime camouflage was first used over the Atlantic on Fw 200 Condors of I./KG 40; He 111s of III./KG 40; floatplane torpedo—bomber He 115s of Kü.Fl.Gr 506; Ju 88s and Bf 110s reconnaissance variants of 3.(F)/123 and such seaplanes as Do 18s or Ar 196s. Coding of Geschwader and Gruppe followed the same standards as in the case of bomber, reconnaissance and transport landplanes — black alpha—

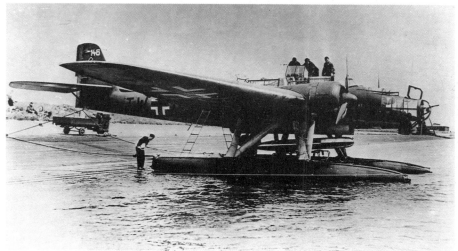

He 115 seaplane in the maritime camouflage of RLM 72/73/65, with black radio code TW+?? on the fuselage and wings, and a white number 146 on the fin. Under the fuselage a training torpedo with a white — red nose (live torpedoes had noses in natural metal).

(P. Jarrett via B. Ketley)

Arado Ar 196A reconnaissance seaplane in the maritime camouflage of RLM 73/72/65 with T3+CI markings of Bordfliegergruppe 196 is taking off from a ship's catapult.

(R. Miczulec coll.)

Four-engined Junkers Ju 290A–5, KR+LA, W.Nr. 0170, in maritime camouflage of RLM 72/73/65. Light side surfaces were blue RLM 65. Balkenkreuze and Hakenkreuze in a reduced form of outlines only.

(R. Michulec coll.)

Mighty nose of a Junkers Ju 290 A-5 of FAGr 5 equipped with FuG 200 Hohentweil radar (1943). Dark fuselage top is a part of the "martime" camouflage of RLM 72/73, fuselage sides in RLM 65 blue. The unit emblem os a sailing ship in a yellow field with black outline is clearly visible.

(P. Jarrett via B. Ketley)

numeric unit and coloured (yellow, red, white, green) individual letters. In the summer of 1941 new maritime units appeared, equipped with maritime camouflaged aircraft: II./KG 40 with Do 217Es, KGr 606, Kü.Fl.Gr.106 and 506 with Ju 88As, Kü.Fl.Gr.906 with He 115s and Bordfliegerstaffel 196 with Ar 196As and He 114s. Two of these units — Kstenfliegergruppe 106 and 506, which exchanged their He 115s for Ju 88s — took part in operations against Allied shipping in the Bay of Biscay. Junkers Ju 88s were painted in grey hues of green (RLM 72/73) on top, while undersurfaces in standard blue (RLM 65) were overpainted black at unit level. Black was also applied on all white elements, such as crosses, swastikas, code letters. One of the 1./Kü.Fl.Gr.506 Junkers Ju 88s, S4+OH, was black on all undersurfaces, and the yellow code letters were overpainted black, leaving just a thin outline. Land bases on the Mediterranean coast were used by maritime aircraft of SAGr 125 and 126 (Ar 196 and Fokker T.VIIIW seaplanes) and SAR units using the Dornier Do 24. Some of the aircraft featured yellow wingtips or white noses and rudders, for example the He 60 floatplanes which were in use for some time.

In the Baltic it was standard practice to use yellow identification elements — fuselage bands and wingtips — in a similar way to that on the Eastern Front in 1941–45. An interesting detail that distinguished the maritime aircraft from their land counterparts was in the painting of propeller blades. While the land aircraft had their propeller blades in black—green (RLM 70) without any blade—tip marking (for example, yellow was used by the Americans and the British); the aircraft in maritime use such as Do 18s or Do 26s featured RLM 70 blades with tips in three colours: yellow (RLM 04), blue (RLM 24) and red (RLM 23).

In the summer of 1940 German pilots forced to bale out over the Channel or North Sea could count on search and rescue aircraft — the He 59 biplanes — or SAR

Fw 200 C "Condor" with clearly visible camouflage in RLM 72/73/65. This was the "maritime", more grey variant of the standard RLM 70/71/65 scheme for bombers.

(R. Michulec coll.)

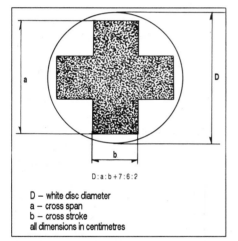

D : a : b + 7 : 6 : 2

D – white disc diameter
a – cross span
b – cross stroke
all dimensions in centimetres

Table No. 2

RED CROSS AND WHITE DISC SIZES AS APPLIED TO SEA AIR RESCUE AIRCRAFT (L.Dv 521/1)									
D	52	70	87	105	122	140	157	175	192	210
a	45	60	75	90	105	120	135	150	165	180
b	15	20	25	30	35	40	45	50	55	60

Fw 200 C–1 "Condor" four-engined bombers saw much success in fighting Allied shipping in the Atlantic and North Sea. They equipped only one operational unit, KG 40; its emblem (globe in a ring) was applied on the fuselage. On the nose tip — "Polaris" in white (each aircraft bore the name of a different celestial body). Camouflage is the maritime colours of RLM 72/73.

(R. Michulec coll.)

boats of the Kriegsmarine. Twin–engined He 59 floatplanes were painted white overall with red crosses in place of the standard black Balkenkreuze, while the vertical tail sported a red band with a black swastika in white circle, the swastika being the "nonmobile" style of the Reichdienstflagge — Reich Service Flag. Forward of the swastika a white Luftwaffe eagle was applied.

Since the aircraft fulfilled a humanitarian role, they did not carry military codes but civil registrations (for example, He 59C–2 of Seenotflugkommando 3, coded D–A+SAM). In spite of that, the British attacked these aircraft, in the belief that they took part in military operations. The Germans then were forced to change the scheme on SAR aircraft by introducing the maritime camouflage RLM 72/73/65 with military radio codes on the fuselage sides, applied normally in black (for example, He

59C–2, W.Nr. 0840, DA+WT, of Seenot-flugkommando 3, or He 59D–1, W.Nr. 2602, NE+UX, of Seenotflugkommando 4). Aircraft used for casualty evacuation (Ju 52/3m, Fi 156 Storch) were also marked only with factory codes on fuselage and wings, and red crosses in white discs.

Their camouflage was at first RLM 02 overall, later replaced by the dark green scheme of RLM 70/71/65. This was not the "maritime" set of colours as the aircraft operated inland, consequently the land set was used instead.

Maritime camouflage of RLM 72/73/65 was also used on the gigantic flying boats, the six-engined Bv 222s used in 1941 by LTS(See) 222, with Geschwader code "X4" (later SAGr 129). The Battle of the Atlantic, gathering momentum since 1941, was fought between the escorts of Allied convoys sailing to Britain and Russia, and joint forces of the Kriegsmarine and Luftwaffe, the latter engaging large forces that operated over the North Sea and Atlantic. Bomber aircraft armed with torpedoes — He 111H–6s of KG 26, Ju 88A–4s of KG 30 and He 115s of Kü.Fl.Gr 406 and 906 —

Table No. 3

TABLE OF ADDITIONAL RLM COLOURS, INTRODUCED IN LUFTWAFFE IN 1941

RLM COLOUR	ENGLISH NAME	ESTIMATED FS 595b COLOUR	ESTIMATED HUMBROL ENAMEL COLOUR
77 HELLGRAU	LIGHT GREY	36492	147
78 HELLBLAU	BLUE	35352	65 + 89
79a SANDGELB	SAND YELLOW	30257	63
79b SANDBRAUN	SAND BROWN	30215	62
80a OLIVGRÜN	OLIVE BROWN	33070	155
80b OLIVGRÜN	OLIVE GREEN	34096	116

attacked with much success the cargo ships loaded with war materiel from American factories. Camouflage of the bombers was in "land", not "maritime" shades (With the exception of the He 115 floatplanes, which wore the RLM 72/73/65 scheme as stand-ard. For example, He 115C–1, 8L+IH, of 1./Kü.Fl.Gr 906). Torpedoes used on the aircraft were unpainted, left in natural metal finish, except for training rounds, the noses of which were finished in red (RLM 23) and white (RLM 21).

An extreme shot - a great BV 222 flying boat overflying an orchard (1940). The "martime" camouflage pattern of RLM 72/73 on upper surfaces.

(MVT via M. Krzyżan)